Written by Zach Breitenbach and Daniel McCoy, the volume *God Conversations* zeroes in on apologetics and discipleship, seeking to equip believers in the process. It discusses an enormous range of topics such as the existence of God and his attributes, the Trinity, the personal claims of Jesus Christ, the resurrection, and the problem of evil. Its overall purpose is to strengthen believers and provide them with both a message and method for addressing unbelievers. Activities such as knowing, doing, and sharing skills are also addressed. It might serve as an all-purpose Swiss Army Knife for Christians!

 —Gary Habermas, Liberty University

God Conversations is an essential guide for Christian parents. It covers a variety of important questions about God and provides thorough and thoughtful answers. The conversations are packed with Scripture and worded in a way to be easily understood by kids, while still providing satisfying answers to tough questions. This is a book that parents NEED in their arsenal.

 —Nicole Stine, homeschool mom and co-author of *Real Life Theology Conversations*

When a student or young person is doubting God or having questions about Christianity, there's nobody in the world I trust more than Dr. Zach Breitenbach. This book will be a treasure for teens, college students, and their spiritual leaders. Dr. Zach, as I like to call him, has a proven gift for connecting deep apologetic truths to seekers and believers of all ages. I've seen firsthand how Zach can guide minds and hearts into the Truth of God's Word, and so I'm delighted that he has taken the time to write his refined thinking in *God Conversations: 20 Discussions for Students on Whether God is Real and What He's Like.*

 —John S. Dickerson, Lead Pastor, Connection Pointe Christian Church, Author of *Jesus Skeptic,* nationally-awarded journalist

In my experience as a mom and also as someone in ministry, teenagers have questions about God, and they want solid answers they can rely on. *God Conversations* doesn't shy away from difficult questions; instead, it helps parents and other influential adults navigate tough issues with teens in a loving and reasonable way. This would be a valuable resource for every youth pastor to have on their shelf!

 —Lindsey Medenwaldt, author of *Bridge-Building Apologetics*

Desperately needed meaningful conversations about God often don't occur because we don't know how to start, what to say, or how to deal with tough questions. This versatile book is the answer! It's written by highly qualified scholars who know how to connect—even with kids. The twenty questions are captivating, and the guidance offered is compelling. Use it with your child, your small group, or your class; but use it. It's a practical tool made of high-quality material.

—**Richard A. Knopp,** Ph.D., Executive Director, Room For Doubt; author of *Truth About God: What Can We Know and How Can We Know It?*

Thoughtful, clear, and incredibly practical. These twenty conversation guides equip parents and leaders to tackle students' toughest questions about God with both truth and tenderness.

—**Bobby Harrington,** Pastor, Author, and Point Leader of Renew.org and Discipleship.org

In world that has many questions about God, whether he is real, and what he is like, Daniel and Zach provide clear and concise answers filled with biblical truth, insights, and wisdom. This is an essential guide for navigating the hardest questions about who God is and why he matters.

—**Andrew Jit,** co-author *Real Life Theology Handbook*

Following Scripture's command to give a reason for the hope that is in every believer, Breitenbach and McCoy offer timely help and substantive answers touching on the essential questions of faith and life. As a teacher of apologetics, I especially appreciate the format of the material. Definitely a book I will integrate into my ministry!

—**T. J. Gentry,** D.Min., Ph.D., Associate Professor of Theology and Ministry, Carolina University real life questions.

God Conversations

20 DISCUSSIONS for **STUDENTS** on **WHETHER GOD IS REAL** and **WHAT HE'S LIKE**

DANIEL MCCOY
& ZACH BREITENBACH

RENƎW.org

Contents

How to Use This Book 11

Section 1 – God's Qualities and Existence **15**

   1. What is God like? 17

   2. When we study the world around us, do we find clues
       for God? 27

   3. When we look within ourselves, do we find clues for
       God? 37

   4. Why does something exist rather than nothing? 45

   5. As we learn more about the world, is there less need
       for God? 53

Section 2 – The Trinity and Jesus as God **63**

   6. So, the Holy Spirit is God, but so is the Father and so
       is Jesus—and yet there's one God? 65

   7. Did Jesus really claim to be God? 75

   8. Is there any good historical evidence that Jesus rose
       from the dead? 83

   9. If it's really true that Jesus rose from the dead, what
       does this mean for my life? 95

  10. How does Jesus' death save me from my sins? 103

  11. People in other religions claim to have experienced
       God. Do they have the Holy Spirit too? 113

Section 3 – God's Justice and Goodness **123**

    12. Is the God of the New Testament the same as the
        God of the Old Testament? 125

    13. How can I trust a God who has killed people in the
        Bible? 135

    14. Why should God get so worked up over sin? 143

    15. What gives God the right to judge us—especially with
        eternal punishment? 153

    16. If we love God as Father, doesn't that go against
        fearing God as King? 161

    17. Will God save a serial killer who believes in Jesus? 171

Section 4 – The Problem of Evil and Suffering **180**

    18. Can we believe in a powerful and loving God when
        the world has so much suffering and evil? 183

    19. How do I deal with the anger and distrust I feel
        because of suffering and unanswered prayer? 193

    20. Is Jesus worth following even when it gets hard? 203

Notes 213

About the Authors 215

How to Use This Book

Welcome, and thanks for picking up our book!

As long as people have been around, they've had questions about God. Is God there? Who is God? What is God like? Does God care about us? Why should we care about God?

Tough questions about God aren't something we need to run from or skim over. Instead, they're chances to have real, meaningful conversations. In this book, we've mapped out twenty conversations, each based on an important but tough question about God. In the conversations, you'll find helpful truths along with engaging questions to think about and discuss. This is meant to help you and others explore the truth about God in honest dialogue.

What kind of relationship are these conversations ideal for? Here are some ideas we suggest (although these are far from the only ways to use this book):

- **Parent-kid conversations.** If you are a parent and you would like to talk with your kid about God, these conversations can help you explore questions about the Trinity, suffering, science and faith, judgment, and other crucial topics. These are written in such a way that middle schoolers and high schoolers can keep up, although it's not limited to that age group.

- **Teacher-student conversations.** If you're a student minister or a Christian school teacher, we think you will find these conversations to be engaging tools for teaching topics to your youth group, class, or small group.

- **Disciple making conversations.** These conversations can be useful for discipling relationships of all ages, whether youth or adults. If you are helping to guide someone spiritually (or if you would like to), you could walk through these twenty conversations together—and one day, that person could lead someone else through them, too.

- **Individuals who have tough questions about God.** This book isn't just great for group discussions—it's also a meaningful read for individuals, including those still exploring Christianity. Each section offers simple but thoughtful answers to big questions and connects you with resources to dig even deeper.

Let's also take a minute and walk through the format of this book. Each of the twenty chapters has 5 sections:

1. **"How would *you* answer the question?"** You'll start the conversation by thinking about the key question that's being addressed. You and the person you're reading along with will first think through how you would answer. Then you will read our answer, which you'll go on to explore throughout the conversation. Feel free to linger on this question until you sense that they are truly wrestling with it.

2. **"Now, let's walk through this answer."** This is the longest section of the conversation. The answer provided at the beginning is now divided into five parts, and you can walk through each of the five parts in one sitting or take it one part at a time at whatever pace works for you. Each part ends with a question for discussion.

3. **"Can you fill in the blanks from memory?"** Now that you've walked through all five parts of the answer, you'll see if you can remember them. Earlier, each part of the answer had a blank to fill in (for example, "Part 1. The God of the ___?") and now you'll check to see if you can remember these key words.

4. **Continuing the conversation.** We have also written a section at the end of each conversation called "Continuing the Conversation." This section includes three parts: Knowing, Doing, and Sharing. These activities help you apply what you are learning, putting it into action. Here is a brief outline of this section:

   a. **Knowing:** Helps you remember and review key takeaways from the conversation.

   b. **Doing:** Reinforces the truths you have learned and helps you put it into action.

   c. **Sharing:** Gives ideas for how to share what you've learned with others or how to invite someone to join the conversation.

5. **Additional resources.** The answers we provide in the twenty conversations are informative but brief. If you want to explore the topic of the conversation even more deeply, we offer some scriptures, books, articles, videos, etc. that will help you. Not every resource listed is in complete alignment with RENEW.org theology, but every resource listed provides help regarding the conversation's subject matter.

We pray you find these conversations helpful and that they provide you with meaningful opportunities for exploring God and knowing him better!

God's Qualities and Existence

What is God like?

1 How would *you* answer the question, "What is God like?"

Here's the answer we'll explore:

> "The God of the Bible is perfectly loving and good, knows all things, has unlimited power, and is the uncreated Creator of all things."

2 Now, let's walk through this answer . . .

Part 1: "The God of the Bible . . ."

When you say the word "God," different people think of different things. One might think of "God" as a bearded person living somewhere in the sky. Others think of "God" as more of a life force than a person, like the Force in Star Wars. But the Bible reveals a different concept of God—one who is perfect and is unique among the world's religions. The Bible is God's Word; it's made up of many books written by different people, but they all fit together to tell one big story that God guided. These writings reveal what God is actually like by telling us things that God has said and done.

But how can we know what God is like? After all, over and over again, the Bible says that God is "holy" (meaning "set apart"). This means God is not like anyone or anything else. In so many ways, he's not like us. For example, we humans were born and will someday die—but not so with God. We are stuck in moment-by-moment time; God isn't. We humans change a lot over time; God doesn't. So, it might seem that God would be hard to understand since he is so great and we are so limited.

But the good news is that God *tells* us a lot about what he's like. And he does this first and foremost by *making* things. By making a massive universe, he tells us that he's really powerful. By making a physical world that runs according to scientific laws, he tells us that he's really intelligent. By putting a sense of right and wrong in our hearts, he's telling us that he cares about what's good. So, even though we will never know *everything* about God in this life, God has told us a *lot* about what he's like–enough for us to love him and relate to him.

Q. What is something that you have made (e.g., something you've built, a story you've written, etc.)? Does it give any clues as to what *you,* its creator, are like?

Part 2: "The God of the Bible **is perfectly loving and good** . . ."

The Bible often calls God our Father. As our Father, he loves us and wants us to treat each other well. One of the things God does in the Bible is give us rules which help us keep from hurting each other. For example, he gives us rules against stealing from each other, abusing each other, and telling lies about each other. When we follow his rules, life is way better for us and for the people we're around. Our Father isn't just someone who loves a lot; his very *nature* is love. As 1 John 4:8 says, "Whoever does not love does not know God, because God is love." First John 3:1a says, "See what great love the Father has lavished on us, that we should be called children of God! And that is what we are!"

Although God is described in the Bible as a father, he's also described as a judge. In Genesis 18:25, God is called "the Judge of all the earth." He is perfectly good and is the ultimate standard of goodness. As Psalm 119:68a puts it, "You are good, and what you do is good." Now, let's think about what a judge does. In a courtroom, the judge hears an accusation against somebody; then he hears the evidence for and against them, and he makes the decision. And the Bible says that, at the end of time, God the perfect judge "will repay each person according to what they have done" (Romans 2:6). This is good news because it means that, in the end, God will bring justice where there has been a lot of injustice and unfair suffering. He will punish evil and rescue his creation.

At the same time, it's not great news for us, because we ourselves have done lots of things we know were wrong and hurtful. In our sin, we have become part of the problem. But here's the really amazing news: God is a judge who offers forgiveness to those who repent and turn to him for mercy. First John 1:9 says, "If we confess our sins, he is faithful and just and will forgive us our sins and purify us from all unrighteousness."

Q. What are some types of injustice and suffering in this world you are looking forward to God bringing to an end?

Part 3: "The God of the _Bible_ is perfectly _loving_ and _good,_ **knows all things . . .**"

It's easy to think about the Bible as a collection of stories about amazing people who followed God and left us good examples to follow. But if we're honest, it's more like a single story in which there's one true Hero, God, and a bunch of people who sometimes follow him but often don't. These followers tend to make a huge mess of things. For example, although Abraham and Sarah were amazing in that they followed God to an unknown land and kept their faith in God through uncertain times, it's also true that they did weird and immoral things like this: Sarah had a slave named Hagar, and when Sarah was unable to get pregnant, she offered her female slave to Abraham so that he could get her pregnant. Abraham did go on to have a son with Hagar, but this only made Sarah jealous.

Sarah then mistreated Hagar so badly that Hagar ran away to the desert (see Genesis, chapters 16 and 21).

Someone saw Hagar by a spring in the desert and struck up a conversation with her. "Where have you come from, and where are you going?" the person asked her. She explained that she was running away from her master who was treating her cruelly. At this point, this mysterious person started describing her future. "You are now pregnant and you will give birth to a son," he said. "You shall name him Ishmael [a word that means "God hears"], for the Lord has heard of your misery." He encouraged her to go back to Sarah and Abraham, explaining, "I will increase your descendants so much that they will be too numerous to count." When she realized who it was who was talking with her, Hagar told him, "You are the God who sees me. I have now seen the One who sees me." Hagar went back, and God indeed blessed her son, Ishmael, and went on to make him into a great nation.

What are some things we learn about God from his interaction with Hagar in the desert? We learn that God sees people when they're alone and mistreated. We learn that God sees their suffering. We learn that God even sees their future and knows what he will do to bless their future. As Hagar said, God is the God who *sees*.

Throughout the Bible, we see that God sees and hears everything, whether past, present, or future. In other words, God literally knows *everything*. That includes everything about *us*. In Psalm 139:3-4, the psalmist prays, "You discern my going out and my lying down; you are familiar with all my ways. Before a word is on my tongue you, LORD, know it completely." This also includes everything about the future. In Isaiah 46:10-11 God says, "I make known the end from the beginning, from ancient times, what is still to come. I say, 'My purpose will stand, and I will do all that I please.' From the east I summon a bird of prey; from a far-off land, a man to fulfill my purpose. What I have said, that I will bring about; what I have planned, that I will do." When Jesus came to earth, he showed that he was able to know the future with startling specificity; for example, he accurately predicted that his disciple Peter would deny Jesus three times before the rooster crowed twice (Mark 14:30).

And yet, even though God knows everything (including everything about us), he still loves us and meets us where we are. As we saw in the story of Hagar, he walks with us and gently guides us toward his better future.

Q. Think of times of loneliness or sadness you have experienced, such as Hagar experienced in the desert. In those times, is it hard to feel like God knows all about you and sees you?

Part 4: "The God of the _Bible_ is perfectly _loving_ and _good_, _knows_ all things, has unlimited _power_..."

God is all-powerful. In other words, there is no to-do list too long or task too big that he can't do it. After all, God created everything. He created the lightning bugs and lightning storms, the molecules and the galaxies. And if we can believe the first words of the Bible— "In the beginning God created the heavens and the earth"—then all the miracles that follow are easy for him. If he created eyes, he can easily restore sight to a blind person. If he created life, he can easily raise a dead person back to life. Miracles are totally possible because the greatest miracle of all has already happened—creating this universe out of nothing (something we'll discuss next in _Conversation #2_).

But if God is all-powerful, then that means he can do _anything_, right? And wouldn't that create a problem? Like, if God can literally do anything, then wouldn't he be able to create a stone so heavy that even he himself couldn't lift it? But then, if he can't lift the stone he created, isn't that something he can't actually do?

Well, the truth is, being all-powerful doesn't mean that God can do things that aren't actually real _things_. For example, a married bachelor isn't an actual thing; that's because a bachelor is an unmarried man, which means he can't be married. The idea of a "married bachelor" is just nonsense—just a contradiction. Likewise, an "odd-numbered even number" is just a contradiction and not something that could possibly exist. In the same way, the concept of a stone that is so big that an all-powerful being can't lift it may sound clever, but it isn't a thing that could actually exist—it's just a contradiction. Think about it: How could there be a stone (which, by definition, is a physical object with a *finite* size) that is too heavy for a Being of *infinite* power to lift? So, no, God cannot create such a stone; but that isn't a limitation on God's power because a "stone that an infinite being can't lift" is simply a contradictory concept that cannot exist (like a married bachelor). As C. S. Lewis said about God, "You may attribute miracles to Him, but not nonsense."[1]

The Bible actually mentions a handful of things that God cannot (or will not) do, even though he is all-powerful. For example, he cannot be tempted by sin, nor can he tempt others to sin (James 1:13). He cannot lie (Hebrews 6:18). He cannot swear by anyone greater than himself because there is no one greater than himself (Hebrews 6:13). Why can't he do these things? It's not because God lacks power; rather it's because they go against his perfect nature. And a God who won't sin or lie because of his perfect nature is a whole lot more impressive than the so-called gods of mythology who were greedy and lustful and were basically humans on steroids. The all-powerful God of the Bible is not only someone we can look up to, but he's someone we can trust.

Q. Imagine your friend says to you, "I don't think God is really all-powerful. The Bible says God can't lie, but even I can do that. So doesn't that mean I'm more powerful than God? . . ." How would you respond?

*Part 5: "The God of the <u>Bible</u> is perfectly <u>loving</u> and <u>good</u>, <u>knows</u> all things, has unlimited <u>power</u>, **and is the uncreated <u>Creator</u> of all <u>things</u>.**"*

God is also the uncreated Creator; that is, God made everything but nothing made God. Does it seem a little strange to believe in something that is uncreated—something that was just already *there*? It might seem strange, but it makes sense given our options. Modern science tells us that the universe hasn't always been here; rather, it came into existence at some point in the past. So, we really have only two options: Either there was nothing there before the universe came into existence, or there was something that was already there. Does it make more sense to believe that *nothing* existed before the universe (so there was nothing there to create it), or that something existed before the universe and was already there to create it? We'll get into this question more in a later conversation (*Conversation #4*). But for now, let's just pause and consider the Bible's answer that God was already there—and has always been there. Psalm 90:2 says to God, "Before the mountains were born or you brought forth the whole world, from everlasting to everlasting you are God." While that may be difficult to imagine, we'll see that it actually makes a lot of sense.

Besides being uncreated, does it make sense for God to be the Creator of *all things*? Wouldn't that mean that God created evil too—things like murder, theft, and pride? One important thing to know about evil is that, even though evil is real, evil isn't so much a *thing* as it is a *corruption* of a good thing. For instance, think of an arm that gets broken. Evil is like the break in the arm. There first needs to be an arm before there is a break in the arm. In the same way, God created a good world which evil breaks apart. God gave us the freedom to do evil and corrupt his good creation. Our freedom is good because it means we can choose to love God and each other, but it also means we can misuse our freedom and corrupt things. So evil is really more of a corruption of a good thing than a thing itself.

So, again, God is the uncreated Creator of all things. And that's where the Bible starts. The Bible tells one grand story which begins with God creating the heavens and earth. He then created humans in his own image to rule over the earth. Yet the humans chose to be their own gods, and soon the world had spiraled into sin and corruption. In response, God did a lot to draw people back to him. For example, he did miracles to show people that he was still there. He sent important messages through his prophets, messages that reminded the people to repent. And yet, the sin problem just kept getting worse. However, all great stories have chapters which are tough to read, and it's just when this story was getting darkest that God did something unexpected: he wrote *himself* into the story. God entered the story as a man, Jesus, who would rescue us from our sins and begin restoring us to our original good purpose.

Q. What do you think people miss out on when they reject the idea of a Creator and believe everything came from nothing, by accident?

3 Can you fill in the blanks from memory?

What is God like?

"The God of the B___ (*Bible*) is perfectly l___ (*loving*) and g___ (*good*), k___ (*knows*) all things, has unlimited p___ (*power*), and is the uncreated C__ (*Creator*) of all t___ (*things*)."

4 Continuing the Conversation . . .

Knowing: Using what you learned from this conversation, how would you describe in your own words what God is like?

Doing: Psalm 150:2 says, "Praise [God] for his surpassing greatness!" Take some time to praise God for what he's like. Try to praise him for at least three specific qualities that he has.

Sharing: Let's say someone told you, "It's nice that you have had experiences with God. But you can't actually know what God is really like. God is too different from us for us to know what he's really like." How would you respond?

5 Additional Resources

Scriptures & Print Resources:
- Scriptures: Exodus 34:5–6; Isaiah 40:28–29; 1 John 4:7–10

- Book: Richard Knopp, *Truth About God: What Can We Know and How Can We Know It?* Renew.org, 2021. This short book shows why we can have confidence when it comes to basic truth about God.
- Book: Norman L. Geisler, *Systematic Theology: God and Creation.* Minneapolis: Bethany House, 2003. This reference book (one volume in a four-volume series on theology) devotes multiple chapters to describing the attributes of God.

Online Resources:

Note: To link to these resources, click the QR code below or go to www.Renew.org/GC

- Article: Daniel McCoy, "10 Biblical Truths About God, Life, and You." This article walks through ten fundamental truths about God and life we find from the introduction to the Gospel of John.
- Article: Paul Huyghebaert, "Who Is the God of the Bible? A Foundational Question We Don't Ask Nearly Enough." This article explores God's creativity, majesty, character, and holiness.
- Video Lessons: William Lane Craig teaches a series on the attributes of God.
- Video Lesson Series (Short): This Reasonable Faith animated video series summarizes the attributes of God.
- The Connection Pointe Worldview Website has a series on the attributes of God.

PRIVACY.FLOWCODE.COM

When we study the world around us, do we find clues for God?

1 How would *you* answer the question, "When we study the world around us, do we find clues for God?"

Here's the answer we'll explore:

> "God reveals himself in creation by speaking the universe into existence, writing nature in the language of mathematics, making the universe just right for life, and designing living things with a complex code."

2 Now, let's walk through this answer . . .

*Part 1: "**God reveals himself in creation . . .**"*

God is the ultimate artist and engineer. The Bible says that when we look at the artistry and complexity of what God has made, it reveals to us his existence and his greatness. For example, King David famously writes, "The heavens declare the glory of God, and the sky above proclaims his handiwork. Day to day pours out speech, and night to night reveals knowledge" (Psalm 19:1–2, ESV).

The natural world, without using words, reveals the magnificence of God. This knowledge of God that we can gain by observing creation is part of what is often called "general revelation." All people (in general) have access to it by observing the world; it can be learned without even reading a Bible. And, as science improves, we are only learning even more incredible detail about God's amazing design.

Q. Read Romans 1:18–20. Have you ever looked at nature and been blown away by its artistry/beauty or engineering/functionality—or both? What did this experience tell you about the qualities of the invisible God?

*Part 2: "God **reveals** himself in **creation** by speaking the universe into existence . . ."*

Christians have always believed that the universe began to exist because the Bible teaches this. From the first verse, we learn that "God created the heavens and the earth" (Genesis 1:1b, ESV). In fact, the Bible is clear that God created the universe without using starting materials. He made it *ex nihilo* (Latin for "out of nothing"). Hebrews 11:3 (ESV) says "the universe was created by the word of God, so that what is seen was not made out of things that are visible." What we see did not come from pre-existing visible stuff. God simply spoke, and there was a universe. Could there be anyone more powerful than a Being who "calls into existence the things that do not exist" (Romans 4:17, ESV)?

Although the Bible teaches creation *ex nihilo*, people throughout history have widely thought (even going back to Greek thinkers like Aristotle) that the universe is eternal and uncreated. But that has all changed. In the last century, overwhelming scientific evidence for the beginning of the universe has poured in.

In 1929, Edwin Hubble looked through his telescope and, by observing distant galaxies, demonstrated that space is expanding. He showed that galaxies are rapidly moving away from each other. This implied that, long ago, everything was closer together and had a beginning point. This idea of a "Big Bang" (i.e., the claim that the universe came into existence and has been expanding ever since) was initially strongly opposed. The Big Bang sounded a lot like the biblical claim that God created the universe. In fact, the atheist astronomer Fred Hoyle coined the term "Big Bang" to make fun of the idea. He wanted an eternal universe.

But as the evidence piled up, scientists widely accepted the Big Bang. In 2003, three scientists demonstrated mathematically that an expanding universe must have had a beginning. Their last names are Borde, Guth, and Vilenkin, so their proof is called the "BGV Theorem." At this point, it is clear that the universe started.

Some Christians believe that God created the universe thousands of years ago (young-earth creationism), while other Christians believe that the universe may be much older. Either way, all Christians believe that God is the Creator. While young-earth believers disagree with modern science about when the beginning of the universe happened (the Big Bang is dated to 13.8 billion years ago), all Christians should be glad that the overwhelming view of science today is that the universe had a beginning. A young-earth creationist can say: "While I don't agree with the typical dating of the Big Bang, modern science does agree with the Bible that the universe began to exist."

And if the universe began to exist, then surely it had to be created by something. It didn't just pop into existence. But what would that "something" have to be like? It must be incredibly powerful to create a universe, and it must also be beyond physical matter and space in order to create it. That sounds a lot like God!

Q. In Romans 4:17, God is described as the One who "calls into existence the things that do not exist." He spoke this massive universe with trillions and trillions of stars into existence. How does knowing that God spoke the universe into existence affect the way you think about God or talk to him?

*Part 3: "God <u>reveals</u> himself in <u>creation</u> by speaking the <u>universe</u> into existence, **writing <u>nature</u> in the language of <u>mathematics</u>** . . ."*

As you sat in your science classes, did you ever wonder why there were all these elegant mathematical equations that described the natural world so perfectly? For some reason, the laws of nature can be described using sophisticated equations with an incredible degree of accuracy.

For example, Einstein's famous $E = mc^2$ shows that mass (m) and energy (E) are interchangeable (two forms of the same thing), with "c" being the speed of light in a vacuum. The equation shows that a small amount of mass can be converted into an enormous amount of energy, as seen in nuclear reactions. But why should there be such a specific mathematical relationship between energy, mass, and the speed of light? That is just how nature is. As the famous astronomer Galileo Galilei put it, the universe "is written in the language of mathematics."[2]

We could look at many such equations (see the Reasonable Faith video on mathematics in the "Additional Resources" section below). What's amazing is that these equations allow us to predict, explain, and understand the natural world with incredible accuracy.

Now if there is no God who designed our universe, we can only say that it is a huge coincidence that mathematics just happens to describe the way the physical world works. Mathematics is the study of numbers, sets, and equations. Numbers (like the number 17) do not cause anything or do anything, so why should they have anything to do with the laws of nature? Why isn't physical reality a chaos rather than having this mathematical order? Yet not only can the world be described by math, but it is described by sophisticated math. And we don't force math to apply to the physical world. It just does. In fact, mathematics has actually been used to predict physical realities even before they were physically detected or proven. For example, Maxwell's Equations predicted the existence of radio waves years before they were experimentally verified by Heinrich Hertz in 1887!

It is much more reasonable to think it is *not* just a coincidence that such mathematics describes the way the physical world works. It is best explained by the existence of an intelligent mind who designed the universe using the language of mathematics and designed our minds so that we can comprehend its order through this language. The universe seems to be designed to be understood.

Q. Galileo famously said that the universe "is written in the language of mathematics." Why do you think God would write the laws of nature using elegant mathematical equations?

*Part 4: "God reveals himself in creation by speaking the universe into existence, writing nature in the language of mathematics, **making the universe just right for life** . . ."*

There is no question among scientists today that the universe is just right for life to exist. Many forces and conditions that are crucial to the possibility of life existing anywhere in the universe just happen to be *exactly* what they need to be to support life. If even one of these were just the smallest fraction different, life could not exist.

For example, if the *strength of gravity* were even slightly stronger or weaker, stars, galaxies, and planetary systems wouldn't form, making life impossible. If the *electromagnetic force* (which keeps atoms together) were stronger or weaker, chemical reactions essential for life wouldn't happen, and stable atoms couldn't form. If the cosmological constant (which works against gravity and affects how fast the universe expands) were even a little different, the universe would either collapse or would expand too quickly for galaxies, stars, and planets to form.

There are quite a few examples like this; we only mentioned a few. But here's the point: Science shows that if these very precise factors were even slightly different, then there could be no life in the entire universe; and the odds of the universe supporting life by chance are *extremely* bad. Think of it like this. Let's play a game where you roll a normal six-sided die, and you must get a six to win the game. What are the odds that you win if you get one roll? You have a 1-in-6 chance (not likely, but possible). But now let's say you have to roll a six not once, but thirteen straight times in order to win. The odds of this happening are only about 1 in 13 billion (worse than the odds of winning a lottery where all 8 billion humans on earth each have a ticket). You probably don't like your odds of winning. Let's say you play this game with me, and I don't just roll a six one time or thirteen straight times. Say I roll a six a billion times in a row. Would you play with me anymore, or would you know I am cheating? Of course you would know that I am cheating! Chance is not the best explanation of that. It surely must be set up to be that way. And yet the odds that all of the key forces and conditions of the universe would line up to allow life to exist are far less likely than me rolling a six a billion times in a row. So, the universe seems to be set up that way as well.

This evidence for the fine-tuning of the universe has impressed even many atheists. The atheist astronomer Fred Hoyle admitted that "a common sense interpretation of the facts suggests that a superintellect has monkeyed with physics, as well as with chemistry and biology, and there are no blind forces worth speaking about in nature."[3] Antony Flew, perhaps the most influential atheist of the last century, actually came to believe in God late in life based on this fine-tuning of the universe. He said, "I believe that this universe's intricate laws manifest what scientists have called the Mind of God."[4]

Q. If you played the die-rolling game with your friend and she rolled a six every time, would you keep playing or suspect that she's cheating (i.e., the die is weighted)? Now, consider that the odds of the universe being perfectly fine-tuned for life are like rolling a six every time for billions of rolls. Given this, do you think it's more reasonable to believe the universe supports life due to random chance or due to design? Why?

*Part 5: "God reveals himself in creation by speaking the universe into existence, writing nature in the language of mathematics, making the universe just right for life, **and designing living things with a complex code.**"*

Finally, science has revealed that there is an enormous amount of information within the DNA of living things. Microsoft founder Bill Gates has written that "DNA is like a computer program but far, far more advanced than any software ever created."[5] Since Gates employs highly-trained programmers to develop his software, that should tell us something about DNA: It comes from intelligence and not random, natural processes. Amazingly, one gram of DNA can store 700 terabytes of data (equal to 5,468 iPhones with 128-GB storage). It is the most efficient information storage system on the planet by far.

While computer code uses two symbols (0 and 1), DNA uses four basic characters (represented by the letters A, T, C, and G). These characters pair up along the double helix of DNA, and the order of these characters forms a code that tells cells how to build and run a living organism. DNA is meaningful instructions, and there are 3 billion characters in your DNA. This is clearly real information! What would you think if you walked downstairs and found a bunch of blocks with letters laid out on the floor that spelled out: "Please wash the dishes before I get home –Mom"? Would you think those blocks fell into place like that randomly? Of course not. You would recognize that there are a lot of blocks, and they align into a meaningful pattern. It surely isn't the result of chance. In the same way, DNA has billions of "letters" of code (based on complex arrangements of ATCG) that form meaningful instructions. It is complex information, and complex information always comes from a mind. If such sophisticated information is at the heart of living things, it becomes difficult to think that life originated apart from an intelligence. How could life even begin without an intelligent designer creating it with this rich information?

Q. DNA holds the instructions for how our bodies function and develop. How does knowing that your body contains such intricate, purposeful information make you feel about your life, your purpose, or your relationship to God?

3 Can you fill in the blanks from memory?

When we study the world around us, do we find clues for God?

"God r____ (*reveals*) himself in c____ (*creation*) by speaking the u____ (*universe*) into existence, writing n____ (*nature*) in the language of m____ (*mathematics*), making the universe just r____ (*right*) for life, and designing living things with a complex c____ (*code*)."

4 Continuing the Conversation . . .

Knowing: Using what you learned from this conversation, how would you sum up in your own words the clues for God's existence that we discussed? Perhaps focus on explaining one of the clues.

Doing: Spend a few minutes outside or simply reflect on something in nature (plants, animals, trees, stars, the ocean, etc.). Write down anything that stands out to you about the order or beauty of the natural world. Then read Psalm 19:1–6 and reflect on how your observations of nature lead you to see evidence of God's design.

Sharing: Your friend asks you, "Doesn't belief in God conflict with science? Science explains the universe without needing a creator. In our advanced scientific age, how can you be a Christian?" How would you respond?

5 Additional Resources

Scriptures & Print Resources:

- Scriptures: Genesis 1:1; Psalm 19:1–6; Psalm 139:13–16; Romans 1:18–20; Romans 4:17; Colossians 1:15–17; Hebrews 11:3
- Book: William Lane Craig, *On Guard: Defending Your Faith with Reason and Precision.* Colorado Springs: David C. Cook, 2010. See chapters 4 and 5, which discuss the origin and fine-tuning of the universe.

Online Resources:

Note: To link to these resources, click the QR code below or go to www.Renew.org/GC

- The Connection Pointe Worldview Website has a series that discusses the fit between Christianity and science.
- Video: A ReasonableFaith.org animated video that discusses the scientific evidence that the universe began to exist.
- Video: A ReasonableFaith.org animated video that discusses how nature is written in the language of mathematics.
- Video: A ReasonableFaith.org animated video that discusses how the universe is just right for life.
- Video: Lee Strobel's *The Case for a Creator* discusses how DNA is real information.

When we look within ourselves, do we find clues for God?

1 How would *you* answer the question, "When we study the world around us, do we find clues for God?"

Here's the answer we'll explore:

"We sense within us a real moral law, which points to God. And without God, the moral law crushes us and wouldn't have authority over us. Plus, we can know God exists by experiencing him."

2 Now, let's walk through this answer . . .

Part 1: "We sense within us a real moral law . . ."

Few things are better than a big scoop of your favorite ice cream. And it's amazing how many flavors there are and how different people prefer different ones. One person may think Cookies and Cream is the best, but another person might prefer Mint Chocolate Chip. Clearly, one's favorite flavor is a matter of personal preference. There is no "best" ice cream flavor that is true for everyone. That's why it would be weird for one person to say to another, "You are wrong about Cookies and Cream being the best flavor!" You can't be wrong about something that is a matter of personal preference.

But not everything is a matter of personal preference. Some things are true regardless of what anyone thinks about it. For example, the earth is obviously a globe—and that remains true even if someone believes it is flat or prefers for it to be flat. So what about morality (what is good and bad or right and wrong)? Is morality the sort of thing that depends on personal opinion (like ice cream preference), or does the truth about it not depend on anyone's opinion (like the shape of the earth)?

When we look within ourselves, we discover a real moral law—a law that's not like our favorite ice cream. Our moral experience tells us that there's a real right and wrong—and it isn't a matter of personal preference. For example, it should be obvious that abducting children and torturing them for fun falls short of the moral law. It is wrong. And if someone thinks there's nothing wrong with this at all, such a person is mistaken. Even though some moral issues are less obvious to us than others, it's clear that morality is not the sort of thing that is purely a matter of personal opinion. Surely someone who thinks that torturing a child for fun is morally acceptable is just plain wrong.

Q. Read Romans 2:14–15. God has written his moral law on our hearts, and we show that we believe in a real moral law by how we react to others' actions. Think of a time when someone stole from you, lied about you, cheated you, or hurt you. Did you believe that person was truly wrong for their actions (and it's not just your opinion), or did you respond by thinking they simply had a different opinion from you and that there was no real right or wrong in the situation?

Part 2: "We sense within us a real moral *law*, **which points to God** . . ."

But where did the moral law come from? What would the source of the moral law have to be like? Well, it turns out that it must come from a being who sounds a lot like God.

First, the source of the moral law must be a personal being (one who thinks and can interact with others). Impersonal things like rocks are not moral decision-makers, so it would be odd for the source of the moral law to be impersonal. An impersonal reality can't establish moral duties or hold human persons accountable for upholding them.

Second, the source must be beyond humanity. If the moral law applies to all humans and rises above human opinion, then it must come from a reality that is beyond humanity.

Third, the source must be unchanging. Otherwise, the moral law that comes from it could change such that murder could be wrong today but right tomorrow.

Fourth, the source must be necessarily good. The moral law can't be randomly made up; the source of this law must be perfect by nature and lay down a law that flows from that perfect nature.

Finally, the source must be eternal. If, for example, love must always be good and hatred always evil, then these laws must flow from a source that has always been there.

Notice that the qualities of the source of the moral law are qualities of God. If atheism were true, how could there be a source of the moral law that is like this? So if our moral sense is correct that there truly is a moral law that is binding on all humans, that's a good reason to believe in God.

Q. Read 1 John 1:5–8. Light often represents goodness in the Bible, while darkness represents evil. How does this passage reveal God as the source and standard of moral goodness?

Part 3: "We sense within us a real moral _law_, which points to _God_. **And without God, the moral law _crushes us_ . . .**"

Even though we sense this moral law inside of us, we all know that we often fall short of living up to it. We realize lying is wrong, and we don't like it when others lie to us. But do you lie? Have you hurt someone physically or emotionally? Or have you lusted? Or thought evil thoughts about someone else? Sadly, it's hard to go through one day without breaking the moral law—even if we try to follow it. We simply lack the ability to fulfill its high demands in this life. Unless God exists and there's an afterlife in which God perfects us, none of us have any hope of fully living up to the moral law. It crushes us.

So if any Christian teaching is obviously true, it is that we are sinners in need of grace. And within our hearts we recognize that the guilt of our evil sticks to us. We sense that our evil really causes us to be filthy, and it needs to be purified and dealt with. We cannot simply brush it aside. For example, even if an abuser is forgiven by his victim, that does not erase his guilt for this evil. And even if he goes to jail, that does not remove his moral guilt. Cleansing of guilt is a deep human need, yet we are powerless to do it. We need the perfect moral lawgiver, who has the authority to deal with our guilt. (In _Conversation 10_, we'll explore how Jesus saves us from our sin.)

Q. Read Romans 3:20–24. The heart of the Christian message is that we are all guilty of sin and cannot fix this on our own. Can you sense in your own life, that you fall far short of living up to the moral law and you are guilty? Explain.

*Part 4: "We sense within us a real moral law, which points to God. And without God, the moral law crushes us **and wouldn't have authority over us** . . ."*

Without God to serve as the ultimate Judge who holds us accountable for our moral actions in the afterlife, the moral law wouldn't mean much. It wouldn't have much of a grip on us. Why care about following the moral law when doing so is costly?

Without God as our Judge, we might still care about our moral actions sometimes. For example, you might decide not to harm someone or steal something or cheat in a situation where you fear being caught and punished in some way. It makes sense to "be good" when it seems to get you ahead in this life.

But doing the right thing is often difficult and costly, so why be good if there's no accountability in the afterlife? Why be selfless when it's easier to be selfish? Why forgive someone when you can get away with revenge? Why accept losing something you want or being inconvenienced just to follow the moral law? Ultimately, without a divine Judge, the moral law is watered down—it loses much weight and significance.

Q. Read 2 Corinthians 5:10. If there were no final judgment from God, how might that affect your motivation to live a moral life, especially in situations where doing the right thing is difficult?

*Part 5: "We sense within us a real moral law, which points to God. And without God, the moral law crushes us and wouldn't have authority over us. **Plus, we can know God exists by experiencing him.**"*

There are great arguments and evidences for God and for Christianity—arguments based on morality, science, history, etc. But if the Christian God truly exists, then we can know he exists even without arguments—simply by directly experiencing him.

The Bible teaches that God is involved in our world. The Holy Spirit, one of three persons/minds of God (explained in *Conversation 6*), is especially active in the lives of Christians as well as non-Christians—guiding, empowering, and transforming us. The Holy Spirit convicts unbelievers of sin (John 16:8) and draws them to God (John 6:44). He empowers believers to be his witnesses (Acts 1:8), helps them to pray (Romans 8:26–27; Ephesians 6:18), teaches and guides them (John 14:26; Romans 8:14), lives within them (1 Corinthians 6:19; Romans 8:11), helps them grow in character (Galatians 5:22–23), and reassures them that they are children of God (Romans 8:16).

So if Christianity is true, then there really is a Holy Spirit who is active in our lives in all of these ways. That would mean the Holy Spirit actually does reassure us that God exists, and he does draw us to God—this is a valid way of knowing God exists. Perhaps you have experienced God through answered prayer. Or maybe God has miraculously done something in your life or brought you out of the pit of despair. Maybe you've been in awe of God from the beauty of creation. Or maybe God has even spoken to you very directly. There are many ways that God reveals himself. A great resource with encouraging true stories of God's supernatural involvement in our lives is J. P. Moreland's *A Simple Guide to Experience Miracles*.

Q. How have you experienced God? Have you ever sincerely asked God to reveal himself to you?

3 Can you fill in the blanks from memory?

When we look within ourselves, do we find clues for God?

"We sense within us a real moral l___ (*law*), which points to G___ (*God*). And without God, the moral law c___ (*crushes*) us and wouldn't have a___ (*authority*) over us. Plus, we can know God exists by e___ (*experiencing*) him."

4 Continuing the Conversation . . .

Knowing: Draw upon what you learned from this conversation about our moral experience and our direct experience of God. You might also think of other clues for God that you find within yourself (e.g., purpose, hopefulness, gratitude, longing for justice, beauty, creativity, etc.). When you look within yourself, what do you think are the most powerful clues that God exists? Why?

Doing: Write a short testimony or story about a time when you personally experienced God in some way (e.g., through prayer, nature, a friend, a life event, etc.). If you don't think you've experienced God, take a few minutes to ask God to help you know he is real.

Sharing: Share with a friend or family member the story you wrote down about personally experiencing God. If you don't have a story, ask a Christian friend or family member to pray for you to experience God in a personal way.

5 Additional Resources

Scriptures & Print Resources:

- Scriptures: Romans 2:14–15; Romans 3:20–24; Romans 7:24–25; Romans 8:14–17; Romans 8:26–27; 1 Corinthians 2:10–12; 2 Corinthians 5:10; 1 John 1:5–8
- Book: William Lane Craig, *On Guard: Defending Your Faith with Reason and Precision.* Colorado Springs: David C. Cook, 2010. See chapter six on Craig's moral argument.
- Book: David and Marybeth Baggett, *The Morals of the Story: Good News About a Good God.* Downers Grove, IL: InterVarsity, 2018. This is a good discussion of moral arguments for God.
- Book: J.P. Moreland, *A Simple Guide to Experience Miracles: Instruction and Inspiration for Living Supernaturally in Christ.* Grand Rapids, MI: Zondervan, 2021. This includes inspiring stories of God's activity in our lives.

Online Resources:

Note: To link to these resources, click the QR code below or go to www.Renew.org/GC

- The Connection Pointe Worldview Website has a series that covers the moral argument.

- Video: A ReasonableFaith.org animated video that discusses how a real moral law points to God.

- Video: Zach Breitenbach goes into more detail on defending a moral argument for God's existence.

- Video: William Lane Craig discusses how the Holy Spirit helps us know the truth about God.

Why does something exist rather than nothing?

1 How would *you* answer the question, "Why does something exist rather than nothing?"

Here's the answer we'll explore:

> "Everything (from ants to God) has an explanation for why it exists: things are either contingent or necessary. There must be something necessary that all contingent things depend upon. Since the universe is contingent, a necessary being like God is needed to explain it."

2 Now, let's walk through this answer . . .

Part 1: "Everything (from ants to God) has an <u>explanation</u> for why it <u>exists</u> . . ."

Have you ever wondered why our physical universe exists instead of nothing at all? It's a deep question—and an important one. Since we're born into this world, we might take it for granted. You might think, "Of course this world exists. Of course we live in this universe. It's all I've ever known." But when you pause to think about it, there has to be an explanation for why the universe exists at all.

Let's think about it this way. Imagine waking up one morning and finding on your bedroom floor a strange, glowing rug that you've never seen before. As you move around it, it changes color. When you step on it, you feel a sudden rush of wind, and everything in your room begins to float. You quickly jump off the rug, and everything returns to normal. Now, assuming you weren't on any drugs, you'd no doubt have the thought: "What's the explanation for this rug? How did it get here?" You certainly wouldn't just accept that it's there for no reason.

In everyday life, we instinctively look for explanations for everything. If you hear a strange noise at night, you'll probably investigate where it came from. Whether we're talking about a rug, an insect, a person, a sound, a planet, the entire universe, or God Himself, it's completely reasonable to think that everything has an explanation. Surely, nothing exists for no reason at all.

Q. What do you think would happen if we gave up on thinking there are explanations behind things?

Part 2: "Everything (from ants to God) has an <u>explanation</u> for why it <u>exists</u>: things are either <u>contingent</u> or <u>necessary</u> . . ."

There are two explanations for why something exists. Everything that exists either depends on something else to exist (it's contingent), or it exists because of its own nature and can't fail to exist (it's necessary). Let's briefly explore each of these.

If something is contingent, it would not exist unless something else caused it to exist. Since it depends on something else, it might have never existed at all. For example, you are contingent because you depend on your parents for your existence. If your parents never existed, you wouldn't be here. Contingent things are all around us. A tree exists because it grew from a seed produced by another tree. Your phone exists because of the materials and engineering that went into it. The painting on your wall, the chair you're sitting on, and the clouds in the sky are all contingent. Even the earth itself is contingent, since it was formed through specific cosmic events.

On the other hand, if something is necessary, it must exist. It does not depend on anything else. While contingent things could have failed to exist or could cease to exist, a necessary being cannot fail to exist—no matter what. Its nature is to exist.

Q. What are some other things in the world that are contingent? Can you think of anything that is not contingent?

*Part 3: "Everything (from ants to God) has an <u>explanation</u> for why it <u>exists</u>: things are either <u>contingent</u> or <u>necessary</u>. **There must be something necessary that all contingent things <u>depend</u> upon . . . ."***

Now, when you think about it, there's no logical way that *everything* can be contingent. There can't be an endless chain of things all depending on something else. We need a starting point for the chain—a foundation that doesn't depend on anything else to exist.

To help explain this, think about how small children often ask their parents "why." Here's an example:

Child: "Why is this tree in the forest?"
Parent: "Because a seed grew into a tree."
Child: "Why did that seed grow into a tree?"
Parent: "Because it was planted in good soil with the right conditions."
Child: "Why is there soil with the right conditions?"
Parent: "Because of the natural processes of the earth."
Child: "Why does the earth exist with these processes?"
Parent: "Because it formed in just the right way in space."
Child: "Why did the earth form in just the right way?"
Parent: "Because we live in a universe with just the right natural laws."
Child: "Why does the universe exist?" . . .

Clearly, this chain of "why" questions can't go on forever, with everything depending on something else. At some point, there has to be a first cause—the starting point of the chain. And this first cause must be necessary. If it were contingent, it would depend on something else and wouldn't be the first cause. But can the universe itself be the necessary thing that starts the chain?

Q. Can you summarize why there can't be an unending chain of contingent things and why the first cause in the chain must be necessary?

Part 4: "Everything (from ants to God) has an <u>explanation</u> for why it <u>exists</u>: things are either <u>contingent</u> or <u>necessary</u>. There must be something necessary that all contingent things <u>depend</u> upon. **Since the <u>universe</u> is contingent** *..."*

In the past, many atheists (people who don't believe in God) considered the universe necessary and eternal. They thought nothing created the universe and that the universe was the first cause for all other things. According to this view, everything in the universe ultimately depends on the universe itself, but the universe just exists necessarily.

However, as we discussed in *Conversation 2*, scientific evidence from the last century has shown that the universe began to exist. And if the universe began to exist, it cannot be necessary; it must have come from something else. This means the universe is contingent—it depends on something outside itself for its existence, something beyond the universe that caused it to begin.

Q. If the universe depends on something else that created it, what sort of qualities must the thing that created the universe have?

Part 5: "Everything (from ants to God) has an <u>explanation</u> for why it <u>exists</u>: things are either <u>contingent</u> or <u>necessary</u>. There must be something necessary that all contingent things <u>depend</u> upon. Since the <u>universe</u> is contingent, **a necessary being like <u>God</u> is needed to explain it.** *"*

So, we've seen that, if everything around us is contingent, then *something* must be necessary—something that exists by its very nature and is the first uncaused cause. And this necessary being can't be the universe itself; it must be something *beyond* the universe.

When we think about what this necessary being must be like, it sounds remarkably like the description of God in the Bible. Since the universe includes all space and matter and time, the necessary being that created the universe must be beyond space, matter, and time. It must be eternal and uncaused—the source of everything that exists. The Bible says God has these qualities. For example, Acts 17:24–25 tells us that God is independent—we all depend on him, and he doesn't depend on us at all. And Colossians 1:15–17 says all created things came from God and are held together by him.

These qualities are exactly what we would expect from God. After all, it wouldn't make sense for something to create God—because if something created him, that being would be God. A "created god" isn't worthy of the name "God" at all. So not only does the Bible teach that God is uncreated and self-sufficient, but we've also seen that this idea makes sense: something beyond the universe, with the very qualities the Bible attributes to God, must be the first uncaused cause of everything else.

Q. Read Colossians 1:15–17 and John 1:3. What do these verses say about Jesus' role in creation and in holding everything together? Why do you think that matters for our understanding of God and the universe?

3 Can you fill in the blanks from memory?

Why does something exist rather than nothing?

"Everything (from ants to God) has an e____ (*explanation*) for why it e____ (*exists*): things are either c____ (*contingent*) or n____ (*necessary*). There must be something necessary that all contingent things d____ (*depend*) upon. Since the u____ (*universe*) is contingent, a necessary being like G____ (*God*) is needed to explain it."

4 Continuing the Conversation . . .

Knowing: Given that God depends upon nothing, and everything depends upon God, how does that affect the way you view God and the way you should relate to him?

Doing: Similar to the chain of "Why?" questions above where a child asks why a tree is in the forest, create your own chain of questions. Eventually, you should come to the conclusion that the chain of questions requires a first uncaused cause.

Sharing: Ask a friend, "Have you ever thought about why anything exists at all? What do you think is the explanation?" In the conversation, share how the idea that everything depends on something else eventually leads to a necessary being beyond the universe, like God.

5 Additional Resources

Scriptures & Print Resources:

- Scriptures: Genesis 1:1; John 1:3; Acts 17:24–25; Colossians 1:15–17; Hebrews 1:3; Psalm 90:2; Psalm 102:25–27
- Book: William Lane Craig, *On Guard: Defending Your Faith with Reason and Precision.* Colorado Springs: David C. Cook, 2010. See chapter 3, which discusses the question of why anything at all exists.

Online Resources:

Note: To link to these resources, click the QR code below or go to www.Renew.org/GC

- Video: A ReasonableFaith.org animated video that discusses why something exists rather than nothing.
- Video: Sean McDowell briefly explains why nothing created God.

As we learn more about the world, is there less need for God?

1 How would *you* answer the question, "As we learn more about the world, is there less need for God?"

Here's the answer we'll explore:

> "Some think that science leaves less room for God and 'evidence for God' just appeals to gaps in our knowledge. But science actually gives positive reasons for believing in God. Also, modern evolutionary theory has not disproved that God is the Creator."

2 Now, let's walk through this answer . . .

Part 1: "Some think that <u>science</u> leaves less room for <u>God</u> . . ."

Science studies the natural world. Through the scientific method, our understanding of how the world works has exploded in recent centuries. And we should all be grateful for the many great technologies and conveniences that come from science. If you like playing video games, instantly talking to friends who are hundreds of miles away, or not having to gather firewood to stay warm, you should be thankful for the scientific discoveries that made those things possible.

Because science is such a powerful tool for understanding the natural world, some people think it's removing all the reasons humans used to have for believing in God. For example, in Norse mythology, Thor (the god of thunder) caused lightning and thunder by swinging his hammer. But now we know that lightning is caused by electrical energy building up and discharging in the atmosphere, and thunder is merely the sound produced by the rapid expansion of air as lightning heats it. Likewise, the ancient Egyptians believed the sun moved across the sky because the sun god Ra carried it in a boat. But now we know that the sun is a star that produces energy through nuclear fusion, and we see it move across the sky because our planet is rotating in relation to it.

So, as science explains more and more about how the world works, does it make belief in God less necessary? The famous atheist Richard Dawkins thinks so: "Gaps [in our knowledge] shrink as science advances, and God is threatened with eventually having nothing to do and nowhere to hide."[6] In particular, he thinks that modern evolutionary theory has explained away the appearance of design in the world. Although it used to seem obvious that living things are carefully designed, Dawkins says evolution has "made it possible to be an intellectually fulfilled atheist" because we can now give a natural explanation for the apparent design.[7]

Q. Even if science can explain how certain things in nature work (like the sun or thunder), can we still think that God designed them? Why?

*Part 2: "Some think that <u>science</u> leaves less room for <u>God</u> **and 'evidence for God' just points to <u>gaps</u> in our knowledge . . ."***

Not only do some skeptics of God (like Dawkins) think science is removing all the reasons *ancient* people had for belief in God, but they often claim that the scientific evidence for belief in God that *modern-day* people give simply points to the remaining gaps in our scientific knowledge. Dawkins thinks that those who believe God designed the world have this mindset: "If you don't understand how something works, never mind: just give up and say God did it."[8] This is often called the "god-of-the-gaps" fallacy. It's a fallacy (a mistaken way of thinking) because it relies on ignorance. It wrongly assumes that if something cannot currently be explained by natural causes, then it must be the result of a supernatural being. It fails to recognize that gaps in our knowledge may eventually be filled by later scientific discoveries, just as they have been throughout history.

But what about the scientific evidences for God that we've discussed already in this book? Do they merely rely on gaps in our knowledge? Do they commit the "god-of-the-gaps" fallacy?

Q. Before reading on, can you think of any scientific evidence that seems to point to God that doesn't commit the "god-of-the-gaps" fallacy?

*Part 3: "Some think that <u>science</u> leaves less room for <u>God</u> and 'evidence for God' just points to <u>gaps</u> in our knowledge. **But science actually gives positive reasons for believing in God . . ."***

Notice that the scientific clues for God that we discussed in *Conversation 2* don't appeal to any gaps in our knowledge at all. Rather, they are based on scientific discoveries that we do know. These clues appeal to positive evidence and not ignorance.

For example, we saw that it's now widely accepted in science that the universe began to exist. It isn't that we're clueless about the history of the universe and just say "God made it." There is a lot of evidence that points to the universe having a beginning. Then, based on this scientific fact, we think about what sort of thing could create a universe. This leads us beyond science and the natural world to the supernatural—whatever brought the entire physical universe into existence is obviously beyond the physical universe. It must be beyond space, time, matter, and energy in order to create those things. It must also be incredibly powerful.

So this isn't like understanding nothing about thunder and saying a thunder god with a hammer is responsible. We start with a scientific fact and then reason to the best explanation for that fact. This is known as "inference to the best explanation," and it's how scientists often work—choosing the explanation that best fits the known facts. In this case, the best explanation for the beginning of the universe is a powerful cause that is beyond space, time, matter, and energy.

Likewise, we appealed to other facts that we know from science, such as how the universe is fine-tuned for life and how DNA is a highly complex and meaningful code that functions like a computer program. These are facts that are widely accepted in science today. We then reason about what best explains them. The odds of the fine-tuning happening by random chance are well understood, and the odds are so astronomically bad that chance is a poor explanation. Design is far more plausible.[9] And DNA is clearly complex and meaningful information. Whenever we see information (in a book, computer program, etc.), a mind is always responsible for it. So, concluding that these things are designed is based on established facts and reasoning based on our repeated experience.

We should also remember that there are non-scientific reasons for thinking that God exists—evidence based on things like morality and personal experience (as discussed in *Conversation 3*). These also appeal to things we know and not merely gaps in our knowledge.

Q. What's the best explanation for the scientific clues we've talked about (like the beginning of the universe or the fine-tuning)? Is it more like following real evidence, or more like making up a story (like saying thunder is caused by Thor's hammer)? Explain.

*Part 4: "Some think that science leaves less room for God and 'evidence for God' just points to gaps in our knowledge. But science actually gives positive reasons for believing in God. **Also, modern evolutionary theory . . .**"*

But doesn't evolutionary theory call into question God's role in creation? Some argue that if evolution can give a natural explanation for the diversity of life (how there are so many different kinds of living things), it removes the need for a designer. Let's take a look at what evolutionary theory actually says and then consider whether it eliminates the need for God.

Modern evolutionary theory tries to explain the diversity of life on earth by a natural process that happens slowly over a long period of time. The theory began with Charles Darwin in the 1800s, who proposed that species evolve through a process called natural selection. Small changes randomly occur within a population of living things (e.g., certain finches have narrower beaks than others), and these random changes sometimes provide an advantage in surviving and reproducing (e.g., the birds with narrower beaks can get to food better). It is called "natural selection" because, in nature, traits that aid in survival are "selected" (passed on from parents to children). Darwin didn't know what caused the random changes, but modern evolutionary theory suggests that they're caused by random genetic mutations (unexpected changes in DNA that happen by chance and can affect how living things grow or function).

Evolution is also said to occur on different scales. *Microevolution* refers to small changes within a species, like the variation in the beak shape of finches. (A species is a group of genetically similar organisms that can mate with each other and have babies that are, when grown, are also able to reproduce. For example, domestic dogs come in different breeds, but they all belong to the same species.) *Macroevolution*, on the other hand, involves bigger changes that can result in the formation of new species. Little changes within a species add up over time to big changes so that an entirely new species emerges. Thus, macroevolution involves all living things sharing a common ancestry: through millions of years of gradual changes, all life forms, from plants to animals, are connected by a long evolutionary history and began with a single-celled organism (the first living thing).

Nobody denies that microevolution happens; there are small differences *within* a species (like skin color or beak shape). But some scientists do question macroevolution—and for good reasons. Nevertheless, some people think that if macroevolution is true, then God isn't needed to explain why living things look designed. If all the different animals and plants resulted from a purely natural process, then we can explain it without God's design. Let's explore this claim.

Q. Are you familiar with these concepts (microevolution, macroevolution, natural selection, random genetic mutations, etc.)? Do you think macroevolution is a challenge to the Bible?

Part 5: "Some think that <u>science</u> leaves less room for <u>God</u> and 'evidence for God' just points to <u>gaps</u> in our knowledge. But science actually gives <u>positive</u> reasons for believing in God. Also, modern <u>evolutionary</u> theory **has not <u>disproved</u> that God is the Creator.**"

Modern evolutionary theory should *not* make us reject intelligent design. Let's briefly consider a few reasons why.

First, we've already seen multiple good scientific clues for God, and macroevolution has nothing to do with them. Regardless of whether macroevolution is true, the beginning of the universe, the fine-tuning of the universe for life, the information in the DNA code, and the mathematical language of the universe all point to an intelligent designer.

Second, even if macroevolution were true, that doesn't explain how the first living cell began. In order for evolution to begin, there first needs to be a living cell with DNA that could copy itself and make new cells. We now know that a single cell is enormously complex, functioning much like a bustling factory with various specialized structures performing many tasks (energy production, waste disposal, communication, manufacturing, etc.). And even the simplest single-celled organisms have hundreds of thousands of base pairs of DNA (letters in their DNA code). The more we learn about the cell and the information in DNA, the more reasonable it is to think design best explains how life began. Evolution does not explain where the information in the DNA of the first living cell came from.

Third, there are significant challenges to macroevolution as a purely natural way of explaining how we got so many different kinds of living things (the diversity of life). We can't cover them all here, but one big challenge is the so-called "Cambrian Explosion." This refers to a period in earth's history in which many major animal groups appear suddenly in the fossil record rather than there being a chain of gradual changes over time. Somehow a lot of new genetic information came about rapidly. Another big problem is that random mutations to DNA code are far more likely to cause damage than anything useful. Just like randomly changing letters in a computer program will almost always break the code and almost never add new functionality, the same is true with DNA.

Ultimately, the case for a Creator is strong. Macroevolution faces significant challenges, and it would not undermine all the great evidence for design even if it were true. In fact, these clues for God—the beginning of the universe, the fine-tuning of the universe for life, the information in the DNA code, and the mathematical language of the universe—would all need to be in place for macroevolution to get started in the first place.

Q. Can you explain in your own words why macroevolution would not cancel out the evidence for intelligent design that we saw in earlier conversations (e.g., the beginning of the universe, the fine-tuning of the universe, and the information in DNA)?

3 Can you fill in the blanks from memory?

As we learn more about the world, is there less need for God?

"Some think that s____ (*science*) leaves less room for G____ (*God*) and 'evidence for God' just points to g____ (*gaps*) in our knowledge. But science actually gives p____ (*positive*) reasons for believing in God. Also, modern e____ (*evolutionary*) theory has not d____ (*disproved*) that God is the Creator."

4 Continuing the Conversation . . .

Knowing: Using what you learned from this conversation, sum up in your own words the idea of the "god-of-the-gaps" fallacy. Also, summarize in your own words the concepts of microevolution and macroevolution.

Doing: Do a role play in which a friend or family member challenges you by making one or both of these claims: (A) "You say there's evidence for God, but you're making the 'god-of-the-gaps' mistake. You just point to things we don't yet understand and claim that God did it." (B) "Macroevolution shows that we don't need God." Using what you learned above, respond to these objections in a practice conversation.

Sharing: Lead a discussion with a group or just one friend (ideally a non-Christian) where you talk through what you learned in this conversation. Invite discussion and raise questions. Share how these ideas connect with your personal faith, and encourage others to reflect on how science and faith fit together.

5 Additional Resources

Scriptures:
- Scriptures: Isaiah 45:18; Jeremiah 10:12; Job 38:1–11; Psalm 104

Online Resources:

Note: To link to these resources, click the QR code below or go to www.Renew.org/GC

- The Connection Pointe Worldview Website has a series that addresses evolution.
- Video: Richard Dawkins explains the "god-of-the-gaps" fallacy, and William Lane Craig argues that science provides clues for God without appealing to gaps.
- Video: Dr. Stephen Meyer and Dr. Douglas Axe illustrate how the information in life could not have been produced by an unguided evolutionary process.
- Video: Lee Strobel's *The Case for a Creator* video series addresses challenges to evolutionary theory.

The Trinity and Jesus as God

So, the Holy Spirit is God, but so is the Father and so is Jesus—and yet there's one God? How does the Trinity make sense?

1 How would *you* answer the question, "So, the Holy Spirit is God, but so is the Father and so is Jesus—and yet there's one God? How does the Trinity make sense?"

Here's the answer we'll explore:

> "The idea that God is a Trinity is unique, but it makes sense. The Bible teaches that the Father, Jesus the Son, and the Holy Spirit are God. Yet the Bible is also clear that there's one God. The Trinity is

the idea of three different persons (or minds) in one Being who is God. The Trinity helps us see how God has always been loving."

2 Now, let's walk through this answer . . .

Part 1: "The idea that God is a Trinity is <u>unique</u>, but it makes <u>sense</u> . . ."

The Trinity confuses a lot of people—non-Christians and some Christians as well. So, if you've ever struggled with the idea that God is a Trinity, you're not alone. It's one of the most unique and mysterious aspects of Christianity. How can God be three-in-one: the Father, the Son (Jesus), and the Holy Spirit?

Some people who reject the Trinity say that it doesn't make sense because they think it means Christians believe in three separate gods that are somehow one God. If that were truly what the Bible taught about the Trinity, then it *would* be a contradiction—three gods can't also be one God. But we'll see that this isn't what the Bible teaches about the Trinity.

Although the Trinity is unlike anything else we experience in the world, we'll see that it's not a contradiction. In fact, we will discover that it actually makes a lot of sense and even helps explain one important quality of God: that God has always been loving, even before he made any creatures to love.

Q. Have you ever avoided thinking about the Trinity because it seemed too hard to understand? Why or why not? Why do you think people from other religions (like Islam) struggle with the idea of the Trinity?

*Part 2: "The idea that God is a Trinity is <u>unique</u>, but it makes <u>sense</u>. **The Bible teaches that the Father, Jesus the Son, and the Holy Spirit are <u>God</u>** . . ."*

Even though the word "Trinity" isn't found in the Bible, the *concept* definitely is. The word "Trinity" is a way Christians describe two important truths that the Bible teaches: (1) the Father, the Son (Jesus), and the Holy Spirit are distinct from each other and are fully God; and (2) there is only one God. Let's first look at the Bible's teaching that each of the three is God. Then we'll look at what the Bible says about there being only one God—and clarify how all of this fits together.

First, the Bible is clear that the Father is God. That's why the apostle Paul says, "Grace and peace to you from God our Father" (1 Corinthians 1:3). He also says it was "God the Father" who raised Jesus from the dead (Galatians 1:1). Even Jesus himself often spoke of "God the Father" (see John 6:27).

Second, the Bible says that Jesus—the Son—is also God. Even though he came to earth as a human, the Bible shows that he is fully God. For example, John 1:1 says, "In the beginning was the Word, and the Word was with God, and the Word was God." Then in John 1:14, it says that this "Word" became human—clearly referring to Jesus. After Jesus rose from the dead, Thomas called him "my Lord and my God" (John 20:28), and Jesus accepted this worship. Jesus also used one of God's names ("I Am"—see Exodus 3:14) and said he existed long before Abraham (John 8:58). The very next verse says the Jewish leaders picked up stones to kill him (John 8:59) because they knew he was claiming to be God. Paul sums it up in Colossians 2:9 when he says that in Jesus "the whole fullness of deity dwells bodily."

Third, the Bible teaches that the Holy Spirit is God, too. In Acts 5:3–4, Peter tells Ananias that he lied to the Holy Spirit—and then says that means he lied to God. This shows the Spirit isn't just a force like electricity. He is a personal Being who can be lied to—and he is God. Jesus also told his followers to baptize people "in the name of the Father and of the Son and of the Holy Spirit" (Matthew 28:19). By putting the Holy Spirit alongside the Father and the Son, Jesus shows that the Holy Spirit is equal to them—fully God.

Finally, the Bible is clear that the Father, Son, and Holy Spirit are not the same—these aren't just different names that all refer to the same person. For example, when Jesus prayed to the Father in the Garden of Gethsemane before he was arrested and crucified, he was not talking to himself. He said, "Not my will, but yours be done" (Luke 22:42), showing that he wanted to be obedient to the will of the Father. Also, at Jesus' baptism, all three (Father, Son, and Holy Spirit) were present at the same time: the Father spoke from heaven, the Spirit descended like a dove, and Jesus was baptized in the water (Matthew 3:16–17). Again, this shows they aren't just names that refer to the same person—they're distinct.

So that's the first part of what gives us the Trinity: the Father, the Son, and the Holy Spirit are each fully God—and they are distinct from each other. Next, we'll look at the second part: how the Bible also teaches that there is only one God—not three.

Q. Did anything in these verses surprise you or help you see something new about the Father, Son, and Holy Spirit all being God? Do you feel like you understand how the Bible shows they're distinct from one another?

*Part 3: "The idea that God is a Trinity is <u>unique</u>, but it makes <u>sense</u>. The Bible teaches that the Father, Jesus the Son, and the Holy Spirit are <u>God</u>. **Yet the Bible is also clear that there's <u>one</u> God . . ."***

Even though the Bible teaches that the Father, Son, and Holy Spirit are all fully God and distinct from one another, it also makes another major point: there is only one God. This is taught all throughout the Bible—in both the Old and New Testaments.

In the Old Testament, one of the most famous verses in Jewish belief says, "Hear, O Israel: The Lord our God, the Lord is one" (Deuteronomy 6:4). For thousands of years, this verse—known as the *Shema* (pronounced "shuh-MAW")—has been central to Jewish faith. "Shema" is the first Hebrew word in the verse and means "hear." Jews recite the Shema in morning and evening prayers, during services, on holidays, and even when someone is dying. The Shema is a powerful reminder that there is only one God. Unlike the surrounding nations that worshipped many gods, God taught Israel from the beginning that he alone is God.

The New Testament repeats this truth in many places. For example, James 2:19a says, "You believe that God is one; you do well." And in 1 Timothy 2:5, Paul writes that "there is one God."

So even though the Father, the Son, and the Holy Spirit are distinct from one another and are each called God, the Bible never teaches that there are three gods. From beginning to end, it's clear: there is only one God. That's why Christians believe in the Trinity—one God who exists as three persons: Father, Son, and Holy Spirit. Next, we'll explain what that means and why it isn't a contradiction.

Q. In Isaiah 45:5, God says: "I am the Lord, and there is no other, besides me there is no God." Why do you think God emphasized throughout the Bible that there's only one true God? Why does believing in one God make a difference in how we relate to God?

Part 4: "The idea that God is a Trinity is <u>unique</u>, but it makes <u>sense</u>. The Bible teaches that the Father, Jesus the Son, and the Holy Spirit are <u>God</u>. Yet the Bible is also clear that there's <u>one</u> God. **The <u>Trinity</u> is the idea of three different <u>persons</u> (or minds) in one <u>Being</u> who is God . . ."**

So far, we've seen that "God is a Trinity" means there is one God who exists as three persons: the Father, the Son, and the Holy Spirit. But what does "person" mean? A person is a conscious *mind*—someone who thinks, feels, makes choices, and relates to others.

A tree or a rock isn't a person because it doesn't have a conscious mind. But humans are persons because each of us has a mind that can think, feel, and relate.

God is one Being, but within that Being are three distinct persons—three minds. You are one being with one mind. But God is one Being who has three minds: the Father, the Son, and the Holy Spirit. Each person of the Trinity thinks, feels, and relates—both to us and to each other. That's why Jesus could pray to the Father (Matthew 26:39). He wasn't talking to himself—he was talking to another mind.

There's no perfect analogy for the Trinity—which isn't surprising, since God is unique. Still, some comparisons can help us get closer to understanding. For example, imagine a three-headed human, where each head has its own mind. It's still one human (one being), but with three distinct minds connected to that human being—each with his own thoughts, name, and ability to speak with the others.

This isn't a perfect comparison (God doesn't have a physical body, and his nature is divine, not human), but it helps us picture how one Being can include three persons (or minds). The Trinity is a unique truth about a God who is beyond anything else in creation—but it's not nonsense. The concept of "God is one Being with three minds" at least makes sense.

Q. Can you explain why it's not a contradiction for God to be one Being who exists as three persons?

Part 5: "The idea that God is a Trinity is <u>unique</u>, but it makes <u>sense</u>. The Bible teaches that the Father, Jesus the Son, and the Holy Spirit are <u>God</u>. Yet the Bible is also clear that there's <u>one</u> God. The <u>Trinity</u> is the idea of three different <u>persons</u> (or minds) in one <u>Being</u> who is God. **The Trinity helps us see how God has always been <u>loving</u>."**

Although Muslims, Jehovah's Witnesses, the Church of Jesus Christ of Latter-Day Saints, and others often say that the Trinity doesn't make sense, it actually makes *more* sense than the idea of God having only one mind. If God were just one person with one mind, how could he always be loving? He couldn't give or receive love until he created other beings like angels or humans.

But the Bible teaches that love isn't just something God *does*—it's something he is. First John 4:8 says, "Whoever does not love does not know God, because God is love." This means love is part of God's nature. It's not just an action he chooses—it's who he is at the deepest level. But if love is that central to who God is, then he must have always been giving and receiving love—even before creating anything.

That's exactly what the Trinity explains. If God is three persons—Father, Son, and Holy Spirit—then love has always existed within God. The three persons of the Trinity have been loving each other from eternity past. So the Trinity helps us make sense of how God can be loving by nature—not just after creation, but forever.

Q. The Trinity shows that God has always been in a loving relationship—even before creating anything. He was never lonely. What does that teach you about how important love and relationships are to who God is and who we are?

3 Can you fill in the blanks from memory?

So, the Holy Spirit is God, but so is the Father and so is Jesus—and yet there's one God? How does the Trinity make sense?

"The idea that God is a Trinity is u___ (*unique*), but it makes s___ (*sense*). The Bible teaches that the Father, Jesus the Son, and the Holy Spirit are G___ (*God*). Yet the Bible is also clear that there's o___ (*one*) God. The T___ (*Trinity*) is the idea of three different p___ (*persons*) (or minds) in one B___ (*Being*) who is God. The Trinity helps us see how God has always been l___ (*loving*)."

4 Continuing the Conversation . . .

Knowing: Write a summary in your own words (just a paragraph or two): Explain what the Trinity is, how the Bible teaches it, and why it matters. Include something that surprised or helped you.

Doing: Create a short summary about the Father, the Son, and the Holy Spirit. For each person of the Trinity: (a) Write 1–2 verses showing that person is God. (b) Write 1–2 verses that describe what this person does or what they are like. (You might use a study Bible or do a web search to find these verses.)

Sharing: Using the summary you created in the "Knowing" activity above, explain to a friend or family member what you learned about the Trinity from this conversation.

5 Additional Resources

Scriptures & Print Resources:

- Scriptures: Deuteronomy 6:4; Isaiah 45:5; Matthew 3:16–17; Matthew 28:19; John 1:1–18; John 8:58–59; John 20:24–29; Acts 5:3–4; Luke 22:42; 1 Corinthians 8:4; Galatians 1:1; Colossians 2:9; James 2:19; 1 John 4:8
- Book: William Lane Craig and J.P. Moreland, *Philosophical Foundations for a Christian Worldview, 2nd edition.* Downers Grove, IL: IVP Academic, 2017. Chapter 31 goes into detail on the Trinity.

Online Resources:

Note: To link to these resources, click the QR code below or go to www.Renew.org/GC

- The Connection Pointe Worldview Website has a series that addresses the Trinity.
- Video: A series of lessons by William Lane Craig that offer a dive deep into the Trinity.
- Article: Matthew W. Bates, "What Is the Trinity in the Bible?" This article walks through who the Father, Son, and Spirit are as revealed in the gospel.

PRIVACY.FLOWCODE.COM

Did Jesus really claim to be God?

1 How would *you* answer the question, "Did Jesus really claim to be God?"

Here's the answer we'll explore:

"Yes! Jesus claimed to be God in multiple ways. He equated himself with God and claimed to have God's ability to forgive sins. He described himself as the unique Son of God and the divine Son of Man."

2 Now, let's walk through this answer . . .

Part 1: "Yes! Jesus claimed to be God in <u>multiple</u> ways . . ."

Tim is a Christian, and his friend Hassan is a committed Muslim. Tim enjoys eating lunch with Hassan, and one day the topic of Jesus came up. Hassan said, "I know you believe Jesus was God, but Jesus himself never actually claimed to be God. After the time of Jesus, Christians decided that Jesus was God. But, even in the Bible, there is no verse where Jesus himself actually says he is God."

Tim was surprised to hear Hassan say this. He knew that Muslims don't believe Jesus is God—they believe Jesus was a prophet, but not divine. This is a big difference between what Christians and Muslims believe. But Tim didn't realize that Hassan thought Jesus himself never even claimed to be God in the Bible. Tim had never been challenged on this point before, and he wasn't sure how to respond. Could it be true? Did Jesus himself never claim to be God?

This is a really important question because it gets to the heart of who Jesus is. For Christians, the belief that Jesus is both fully human and fully God is central to their faith. This teaching, known as the incarnation, means that Jesus existed eternally as God before coming to earth as a human being. Even though he lived as a man, he remained fully God.

So, in this conversation, let's explore multiple ways that Jesus claimed to be God.

Q. Based on what you already know (before reading the rest of this conversation), how would you respond to Hassan if you were in Tim's shoes? Can you think of anything Jesus said or did in the Bible that makes it clear he saw himself as God?

*Part 2: "Yes! Jesus claimed to be God in <u>multiple</u> ways. **He <u>equated</u> himself with God** . . ."*

One way Jesus made it clear that he saw himself as God is by saying things that equated himself with God. One of the most powerful examples of this is found in John 8:58. Leading up to this, in verse 54, Jesus tells the Jewish religious leaders that the God they worship "glorifies" him (gives him special honor). Then, in verse 58, Jesus makes an extraordinary claim: "before Abraham was, I am." This seemed like a crazy statement to make because Abraham lived nearly 2,000 years before Jesus was born! In this statement, Jesus not only claimed to have existed long before his earthly birth, but he also used the divine name "I Am," which God used in Exodus 3:14 when he revealed himself to Moses at the burning bush.

The Jewish leaders immediately understood what Jesus was saying. He was claiming to be God—saying he existed long before his birth and applying God's name to himself. This is why they reacted by trying to stone him (verse 59); they saw his words as blasphemous because Jesus was clearly equating himself with God. Blasphemy (disrespecting God), in Jewish law, was considered a serious offense, and claiming to be God was punishable by death (Leviticus 24:16). This lines up with what the Old Testament said about the Messiah: Isaiah 9:6 calls him "Mighty God" and "Eternal Father," and Micah 5:2 says he existed from eternity, even though he would be born in Bethlehem. Jesus showed that these prophecies were about him.

Another moment where Jesus equates himself with God is in John 20:24–29. After Jesus' resurrection, Thomas, one of his disciples, at first doubted the other disciples' claim that they had seen Jesus alive. But later, Jesus appears to Thomas, and Thomas immediately believes in Jesus and worships him, saying, "My Lord and my God!" Did Jesus get upset with Thomas for calling him God? No. Instead, he accepted this worship and told Thomas that he should have believed sooner.

Here's one more place where Jesus makes himself equal to God. In Matthew 13:41, Jesus says, "The Son of Man will send his angels, and they will gather out of his kingdom all causes of sin and all law-breakers." The "Son of Man" is a title Jesus frequently used for himself (more on that in a moment), so Jesus is claiming the authority to send angels. He's claiming God's angels are his own. Only God has the power to send angels for such a judgment.

Q. What would you think about someone who claimed to have existed thousands of years before they were born, accepted being worshipped as God, and believed God's angels were his own? What kind of person would this be if he weren't actually God? Why?

*Part 3: "Yes! Jesus claimed to be God in <u>multiple</u> ways. He <u>equated</u> himself with God **and claimed to have God's ability to <u>forgive</u> sins** . . ."*

Another major way that Jesus claimed to be God is by forgiving sins, which is something only God can do. In Mark 2:1–12, a man who was paralyzed and couldn't walk was brought to Jesus. The man had faith that Jesus could heal him. But instead of immediately healing the man's paralyzed legs, Jesus responded to the man's faith by saying, "Son, your sins are forgiven" (verse 5).

Some Jewish leaders who heard Jesus say this saw Jesus' claim to forgive the man's sins as blasphemy. This is because they knew that only God has the authority to forgive sins (verse 7). By claiming to have this authority, Jesus was claiming to be God.

So, Jesus said to them that he would prove he had the authority to forgive sins by healing the man's paralyzed legs. Anyone can claim to be God, and anyone can say they are able to forgive sins. But not just anyone can heal a paralyzed man's legs and back up such claims. So, Jesus healed the man right in front of their eyes! This amazed the crowd, and it proved to them that Jesus wasn't making empty claims. This miracle demonstrated that he truly had the authority of God to forgive sins.

Q. Read Mark 2:1–12, Isaiah 43:25, and Psalm 103:12. If your friend says Jesus was just a good teacher and not God, how would you use Mark 2 to show that Jesus must be more than a human teacher? Why is it significant that Jesus claimed to forgive sins—something only God can do, as seen in Isaiah 43:25 and Psalm 103:12?

*Part 4: "Yes! Jesus claimed to be God in multiple ways. He equated himself with God and claimed to have God's ability to forgive sins. **He described himself as the unique Son of God** . . ."*

Jesus also showed that he considered himself to be God by calling himself the unique "Son of God." He didn't just claim to be one of God's sons and daughters (as all humans are "children of God"), and he didn't claim to be just another prophet or messenger of God. He claimed to be the only unique Son of God, with a special relationship and authority that no one else shares.

For example, in Mark 12:1–9, Jesus tells a parable (a story meant to illustrate a point) in which he portrays himself as way more than just another prophet that God sent to speak to the people. He describes himself as God's final—and most important—messenger who came to us with a special mission and with special authority after all the prophets were rejected. He describes himself as God's special Son.

Similarly, in Matthew 11:27, Jesus says that he is the only one who has a deep, direct knowledge of God the Father: "All things have been handed over to me by my Father, and no one *knows* the Son except the Father, and no one *knows* the Father except the Son and anyone to whom the Son chooses to reveal him." The word Jesus uses for "knows" is *epiginosko*—a Greek word that means to know by experience or through direct relationship. Jesus is saying that his connection with the Father is unique. He is not just another child of God, but the special Son of God.

Q. In Hebrews 1:3, Jesus is called the "exact representation" of God's being. What does this tell you about the authority and power of Jesus when he calls himself the "Son of God"? How does this understanding of Jesus affect your faith?

Part 5: "Yes! Jesus claimed to be God in <u>multiple</u> ways. He <u>equated</u> himself with God and claimed to have God's ability to <u>forgive</u> sins. He described himself as the <u>unique</u> Son of <u>God</u> **and the <u>divine</u> Son of <u>Man</u>.***"*

In the Bible, Jesus called himself "the Son of Man" more than any other title (over 80 times in the Gospels). Many assume that Jesus used this title to emphasize his humanity. But, while it's true that Jesus is human, this title actually points to the fact that he is God.

When Jesus calls himself "the Son of Man," he's referring to Daniel 7:13–14, where the prophet Daniel describes a vision of "one like a son of man" who comes on the clouds, ruling over all people with eternal authority. The imagery of coming on the clouds represents divine majesty, and only God can have an eternal kingdom.

It's clear that Jesus is referring to this passage in Daniel when he calls himself "the Son of Man." We see this in his trial in front of the Jewish High Priest (Mark 14:53–65) where he was condemned of blasphemy and handed over to the Romans to be crucified. The High Priest asks Jesus if he is the Christ (the Jewish Messiah) and the Son of God (verse 61). Jesus replies by saying "I am," and then adds that "you will see the Son of Man seated at the right hand of Power, and coming with the clouds of heaven" (verse 62). So, Jesus directly identifies himself as the divine "Son of Man" from Daniel 7, who will come to judge and reign with eternal authority. The High Priest knew what Jesus was saying, and he immediately accused Jesus of blasphemy (verses 63–64).

But Jesus wasn't guilty of blasphemy if he truly is God. So, how do we know if Jesus is a blasphemer or the true Son of God? If Jesus rose from the dead, then God confirmed that Jesus was telling the truth about his identity. This leads us into the next topic: the resurrection.

Q. Read Mark 14:61–64. How does the High Priest's reaction show that Jesus was claiming to be God?

3 Can you fill in the blanks from memory?

Did Jesus really claim to be God?

"Yes! Jesus claimed to be God in m___ (*multiple*) ways. He e___ (*equated*) himself with God and claimed to have God's ability to f___ (*forgive*) sins. He described himself as the u___ (*unique*) Son of G___ (*God*) and the d___ (*divine*) Son of M___ (*Man*)."

4 Continuing the Conversation . . .

Knowing: Using what you learned from this conversation, create a summary sheet with five ways Jesus claimed to be God. For each of these five ways, include a Bible verse and briefly explain what it means.

Doing: Do a role play with a parent or friend where the other person doubts that Jesus ever claimed to be God and you explain ways that Jesus did claim to be God. Use the examples from the summary sheet you created above and explain why these are significant.

Sharing: Talk to a non-Christian friend about how Jesus claimed to be God. Or, using your summary sheet from the "Knowing" section above, teach a lesson at church or create a social media post where you help others see that Jesus claimed to be God.

5 Additional Resources

Scriptures & Print Resources:
- Scriptures: Daniel 7:13–14; Matthew 11:27; Matthew 16:13–17; Matthew 13:41; Mark 2:1–12; Mark 12:1–9; Mark 14:53–65; John 8:48–59; John 20:24–29
- Book: William Lane Craig, *On Guard: Defending Your Faith with Reason and Precision.* Colorado Springs: David C. Cook, 2010. See chapter 8 on the historical Jesus.

Online Resources:

Note: To link to these resources, click the QR code below or go to www.Renew.org/GC

- The Connection Pointe Worldview Website has a series that covers Jesus' identity and personal claims.

- Video: This ReasonableFaith.org animated video discusses how Jesus really claimed to be the Messiah, Son of God, and Son of Man.

- Article: Megan Rawlings, "Is Jesus God? A Narrative Journey into the Evidence." This article uses a hypothetical conversation to walk through evidence that Jesus and his disciples believed him to be divine.

- Article and video: The "Got Questions" website provides some good Bible references to show Jesus claimed to be God.

Is there any good historical evidence that Jesus rose from the dead?

1 How would *you* answer the question, "Is there any good historical evidence that Jesus rose from the dead?"

Here's the answer we'll explore:

"Multiple historical facts point to Jesus' resurrection, including: Jesus was crucified to death by the Romans; his empty tomb was discovered; many people claimed to see appearances of Jesus after he died; and Jesus' disciples sincerely believed in his resurrection. The best explanation of these facts is that Jesus truly resurrected."

2 Now, let's walk through this answer . . .

Part 1: "Multiple historical <u>facts</u> point to Jesus' resurrection, including: Jesus was <u>crucified</u> to death by the Romans . . ."

Have you ever played Jenga? That game is really stressful! When it's your turn, you have to pull out one block without making the entire structure tumble to the ground. If everything crashes down, you lose.

Imagine a huge tower of Jenga blocks, all balanced precariously on one block at the bottom. If that bottom block shifts or falls, the whole tower collapses. If we think of that tower as representing Christianity, then the block at the bottom that holds everything up is the resurrection of Jesus. If Jesus didn't really rise from the dead 2,000 years ago, then Christianity falls apart (1 Corinthians 15:16–17). That's how important the resurrection is—the truth of the Christian faith *entirely depends* on this one historical event.

But here's the good news for Christianity: the block holding up the tower is incredibly secure! There are multiple historical facts related to Jesus' resurrection that the vast majority of historians (even non-Christian historians) believe are true. So, when you're in faith-related conversations with your non-Christian friends, pointing to these facts can be pretty powerful because nobody can say, "You only accept these 'facts' because you believe the Bible." You can share that even scholars who don't accept the Bible as God's Word think these facts are true on the basis of their historical evidence.

We will briefly discuss just four of these historical facts about Jesus, noting some reasons why historians widely accept them. Then we'll see that these four facts alone provide a strong case that Jesus rose from the dead; that's because Jesus' resurrection is the best explanation of these facts.

Here's the first fact: the Romans crucified Jesus to death. Did you know that you'd have a hard time finding any historical scholars today who deny that Jesus really existed or that he was crucified to death by the Romans? Bart Ehrman, a skeptical Bible scholar who does not even believe in God, wrote a book called *Did Jesus Exist?* that argues that Jesus clearly lived and that we can know things about Jesus. In this book, Ehrman says "virtually all scholars" who study the ancient world (whether they are Christian or not) agree that Jesus "was a Jewish man, known to be a preacher and teacher, who was crucified (a Roman form of execution) in Jerusalem during the reign of the Roman emperor Tiberius, when Pontius Pilate was the governor of Judea."[10] So maybe you have friends who doubt that Jesus existed, or you've seen a TikTok video where someone claims that we can't know if Jesus lived or was crucified. But that's not what professional historical scholars believe.

Why is the fact that Jesus lived and was crucified to death by the Romans one of the most certain facts of history? Ehrman says we have at least fifteen different sources that talk about Jesus' crucifixion within one hundred years after he died.[11] For example, a Roman historian named Tacitus lived in the first century and wrote in his *Annals* about how Jesus was executed during the reign of Emperor Tiberius by Pontius Pilate. And a Jewish historian named Josephus, who also lived in the first century, writes in his *Antiquities of the Jews* that Jesus was crucified by Pilate after the Jewish leaders accused Jesus. These details about the death of Jesus do not come from the Bible or even from Christians, and yet they agree with how the Bible said Jesus died.

Q. Did you know that in the Muslim holy book, the Koran, it says that Jesus was never crucified? (See chapter 4, verses 157–158.) As we've seen, this goes against what virtually all historians today believe about Jesus. How might this fact be useful in witnessing to a Muslim friend?

*Part 2: "Multiple historical <u>facts</u> point to Jesus' resurrection, including: Jesus was <u>crucified</u> to death by the Romans; **his empty <u>tomb</u> was discovered**..."*

A second historical fact is that Jesus was buried in a tomb that later went empty. Think about it this way: If it wasn't clear what happened to Jesus' body after he was crucified, it would be hard to have confidence that he rose from the dead. What if we didn't know whether his body was thrown into a common grave with criminals or even fed to animals? Early Christians claimed that Jesus physically rose from the dead—the same body that died came back to life. But without the body's disappearance from a known burial site, this claim would be hard to believe. So, the empty tomb is crucial to the resurrection story.

Fortunately, there are multiple lines of evidence supporting the empty tomb. Let's look at a few of them.

First, there's strong evidence that Jesus was buried in a tomb that was well-known, so everyone could go to it and check to see if the body was in there. All four Gospels (Matthew 27:57–60; Mark 15:43–46; Luke 23:50–53; John 19:38–42) mention that a man named Joseph of Arimathea, a member of the Sanhedrin (the high court of the Jews that had Jesus crucified), buried Jesus in his tomb. It's the only story we have from the first century about what happened to Jesus, and it's unlikely that the early Christians would have made this up—especially because Joseph's role would have been embarrassing to them. While Jesus' disciples hid in fear, this guy on the Jewish high court had the courage to get Jesus' body from the Romans and bury it.

Why admit this, unless it was true? Plus, why make up that a specific Jewish leader buried Jesus when the Jews could easily disprove this? Members of the Sanhedrin were well-known leaders of the Jewish people, and everyone would know who Joseph was. If he didn't bury Jesus, Christians could never get away with making this up.

So, since there's good reason to believe the location of Jesus' tomb was known to everyone, the body had to be missing from the tomb. Nobody in Jerusalem (where Jesus died and where Christianity began) would accept that Christianity is true if a dead body was still in Joseph's tomb.

A second piece of evidence for the empty tomb is that the Jewish leaders themselves—those who opposed Christianity—had to admit the tomb was empty. In Matthew 28:11–15, Matthew records that after Jesus' resurrection, the Jewish leaders bribed the soldiers who had guarded the tomb to spread a story that the disciples had stolen Jesus' body. Matthew says the Jewish leaders spread this story widely, and it wouldn't help Matthew to make this up since his first-century readers would know whether or not this story was really being widely spread.

Of course, if the body had been stolen, then the tomb would be empty. So the Jewish leaders were admitting the body wasn't in the tomb. Historians see this as an important clue: If the tomb had not been empty, the enemies of Christianity could have simply pointed to Jesus' body and ended the whole debate. Instead, they had to come up with an alternative explanation, even though the empty tomb itself was undeniable. If an enemy admits something that would benefit the other side, it likely happened. The Jewish leaders denied the resurrection, but they apparently couldn't deny the empty tomb.

A third piece of evidence for the empty tomb is that all four Gospels say that the first witnesses to the empty tomb were women (Matthew 28:1–10, Mark 16:1–8, Luke 24:1–12, John 20:1–18). Why does this matter? In first-century Israel, women had a much lower status than men. The Jewish historian Josephus even writes that women's testimonies were not considered valid in a court of law.[12] So, if the early Christians were just making up the story of the empty tomb to convince others, they would have chosen men to be the ones to discover the tomb. Since men's testimonies were taken far more seriously in that culture, the story would have been more believable. The fact that the Gospels say women were the first to find the tomb is a strong indication that this is what happened—the story is authentic.

Q. Would anyone have believed Christianity is true if the body of Jesus had not disappeared? What do you think is the strongest evidence for the empty tomb out of the evidences mentioned here?

*Part 3: "Multiple historical facts point to Jesus' resurrection, including: Jesus was crucified to death by the Romans; his empty tomb was discovered; **many people claimed to see appearances of Jesus after he died** . . ."*

Our third historical fact is that many people—both believers and skeptics—claimed to have seen Jesus alive after he died. One key reason historians accept this is the early Christian creed that Paul quotes in 1 Corinthians 15:3–7. (A creed is a short, memorized statement of important beliefs.) This creed lists various witnesses who saw Jesus after his death. Here's the creed Paul received and wrote down in 1 Corinthians:

> "For what I received I passed on to you as of first importance: that Christ died for our sins according to the Scriptures, that he was buried, that he was raised on the third day according to the Scriptures, and that he appeared to Cephas, and then to the Twelve. After that, he appeared to more than five hundred of the brothers and sisters at the same time, most of whom are still living, though some have fallen asleep. Then he appeared to James, then to all the apostles." (1 Corinthians 15:3–7)

Historians widely agree that Paul was a real person and didn't make this creed up; he was passing along a belief already held by Christians, and the creed was likely being recited within just a few years of Jesus' death.[13]

This creed is valuable because it gives us insight into the beliefs of the earliest Christians—those who were closest to the events. Paul himself likely received this creed within five years of Jesus' death, giving us an early and reliable source for the claim of the resurrection.[14]

Let's take a look at some of these witnesses and see why historians believe they really did claim to see Jesus alive.

First, the creed (verse 5) mentions Jesus appearing to Peter (also called Cephas). Virtually all scholars agree that Peter, one of Jesus' closest followers, claimed to have seen the risen Jesus. Why? Because historians accept that Paul knew Peter and spent time with him, as Paul writes in Galatians 1:18. (Galatians is an undisputed letter of Paul.) This personal connection gives us confidence that Paul could confirm Peter's testimony.

Next, the creed mentions an appearance to "the Twelve," a title for the innermost disciples who followed Jesus.[15] Both this creed and two Gospel accounts (Luke 24:36–42; John 20:19–20) mention this appearance. Again, Paul definitely knew members of the Twelve (like Peter), so Paul could confirm this appearance.

Third, the creed refers to an appearance to over 500 people at once. This is a powerful claim. If 500 people saw the same thing, it's hard to dismiss. Paul emphasizes that many of these people were still alive at the time of his writing, so his readers could check with them to confirm the story.

Another witness mentioned in the creed is James, the half-brother of Jesus. During Jesus' ministry, James didn't believe in him (John 7:1–10). Yet, after Jesus died, James became a leader in the early Christian church (Galatians 1:19; Galatians 2:9). What changed? Paul tells us that James saw the resurrected Jesus. If I saw my brother come back from the dead, that would get my attention too! This is huge because it's hard to explain why someone would go from being a skeptic to being a Christian leader unless something big happened. Since Paul personally knew James (Galatians 1:18-19), he could confirm that James really claimed to see this appearance.

Finally, after quoting the creed, Paul adds his own name to the list of witnesses (1 Corinthians 15:8–11). As someone who once killed Christians, Paul's conversion is one of the most dramatic stories of transformation in history. He claims that his encounter with the risen Jesus completely changed his life.

Even skeptical scholars, like Bart Ehrman, admit that these witnesses really claimed to see Jesus alive after his death. Ehrman writes, "Why, then, did some of the disciples claim to see Jesus alive after his crucifixion? I don't doubt at all that some of the disciples claimed this. . . . Paul, writing about twenty-five years later, indicates that this is what they claimed, and I don't think he is making it up. And he knew at least a couple of them, whom he met just three years after the event (Galatians 1:18–19)."[16]

Q. Read 1 Corinthians 15:3–8. Do you think it is significant that Jesus appeared to skeptics of Christianity (like James and Paul) and large groups (like the 500)? How does the variety of witnesses strengthen the case for the resurrection?

Part 4: "Multiple historical <u>facts</u> point to Jesus' resurrection, including: Jesus was <u>crucified</u> to death by the Romans; his empty <u>tomb</u> was discovered; many people claimed to see <u>appearances</u> of Jesus after he died; **and Jesus' disciples <u>sincerely</u> believed in his resurrection** *. . ."*

Our fourth and final historical fact is that the earliest disciples of Jesus sincerely believed he rose from the dead. Scholars don't think these disciples were simply making it up. Why? Well, the disciples weren't gaining fame, fortune, or power by believing in Jesus' resurrection. Instead, they were getting persecuted and often killed. While we don't know exactly how many disciples died for their beliefs, we know that some did—and we know that all of them put themselves at risk of dying.

It takes a lot of commitment to be willing to die for something. Think about it. How many beliefs would you be willing to die for? And it would be *very surprising* for anyone to die for something that they *knew for sure* was false. The disciples either saw the risen Jesus or they didn't. They didn't have to rely on anyone else's testimony—they knew, personally, whether it was true. If they didn't see the risen Jesus, then why suffer or die for this lie? The fact that the disciples put themselves at such peril for this belief makes it clear that they truly did believe it.

Q. In Acts 5:40–42, the apostles were beaten and ordered not to speak about Jesus anymore, yet they continued to preach with joy. Similarly, in Acts 12:1–2, the apostle James was willing to die for his faith. If the resurrection never happened, what could have motivated them to suffer and even die for something they knew was a lie?

Part 5: "Multiple historical <u>facts</u> point to Jesus' resurrection, including: Jesus was <u>crucified</u> to death by the Romans; his empty <u>tomb</u> was discovered; many people claimed to see <u>appearances</u> of Jesus after he died; and Jesus' disciples <u>sincerely</u> believed in his resurrection. **The best <u>explanation</u> of these facts is that Jesus truly <u>resurrected</u>."**

Now, let's look again at the four widely-accepted historical facts we've covered. Can you think of a natural (or non-supernatural) explanation that would explain all four facts well? Over the years, people have proposed different theories, trying to explain away the facts without saying Jesus rose from the dead. Some of the theories include:

- Maybe Jesus fainted on the cross, and the Romans took him off the cross thinking he was dead. Then he later woke up and appeared to people.
- Maybe the disciples stole the body and lied about the resurrection.
- Or maybe people hallucinated seeing Jesus alive.

But the truth is, there's no non-supernatural theory that fits the facts well. Scholars have not widely accepted any of them. Let's just consider the three theories mentioned above.

The fainting theory doesn't work because the Romans were experts in crucifixion. Their job was to make sure the person died, and the Jewish leaders wanted Jesus dead. It's incredibly unlikely that Jesus could have survived the cross. Even if he somehow did survive, his physical condition would have been so bad that he would never have convinced anyone he had supernaturally risen from the dead.

The stolen body theory fails because it doesn't explain the appearances of Jesus (especially to skeptics like Paul or James). It also doesn't account for the fact that the disciples were sincere in their belief and willing to die for it.

And the hallucination theory doesn't work because hallucinations occur only in one's mind. They are not experienced by groups, and yet groups of people saw Jesus. Plus, hallucinations don't explain how the tomb ended up empty.

There are other theories we could examine, but none of them account for all the facts as well as the resurrection of Jesus does. If Jesus truly rose from the dead, it makes perfect sense of the four facts we've discussed. Unless there's good evidence that there's no God who could do such a miracle (contrary to what we've already argued), the best explanation for the historical facts is that Jesus really did rise!

Q. Can you think of a theory that would explain all four historical facts well? Why might some people struggle with the idea of a miracle like the resurrection, even when historical evidence points to it?

3 Can you fill in the blanks from memory?

Is there any good historical evidence that Jesus rose from the dead?

"Multiple historical f___ (*facts*) point to Jesus' resurrection, including: Jesus was c___ (*crucified*) to death by the Romans; his empty t___ (*tomb*) was discovered; many people claimed to see a___ (*appearances*) of Jesus after he died; and Jesus' disciples s___ (*sincerely*) believed in his resurrection. The best e___ (*explanation*) of these facts is that Jesus truly r___ (*resurrected*)."

4 Continuing the Conversation . . .

Knowing: Using what you learned from this conversation and the additional resources below, practice explaining to a family member or friend how most scholars who study the life of Jesus (even non-Christians) believe the four historical facts we discussed. Then, try to summarize the evidence for each fact.

Doing: After doing the "Knowing" activity to gain practice, do a role-play exercise where you explain the historical evidence supporting the resurrection, and a friend tries asking you questions or tries to defend a non-supernatural theory (like the fainting or stolen body theory). Afterward, discuss how the conversation went.

Sharing: After practicing by doing the above two activities, share the evidence for the resurrection with someone who doesn't know it. Ideally, share it with a non-Christian. Or lead a discussion group where you share it with others at church.

5 Additional Resources

Scriptures & Print Resources:
- Scriptures: John 18–20; Acts 2; Acts 5:17–42; Acts 12:1–5; 1 Corinthians 15:1–24; Galatians 1:11–24; Romans 1:1–6; 1 Peter 1:3–9
- Book: William Lane Craig, *On Guard: Defending Your Faith with Reason and Precision.* Colorado Springs: David C. Cook, 2010. See chapter 9 on evidence for Jesus' resurrection.
- Book: Gary R. Habermas, *The Risen Jesus and Future Hope.* Lanham, MD: Rowman & Littlefield, 2003. This isn't Habermas's most scholarly work on the resurrection (for that, see Volume 1 of his 2024 *On the Resurrection*), but chapter 1 sums up well his "minimal facts" case for the resurrection.

Online Resources:

Note: To link to these resources, click the QR code below or go to www.Renew.org/GC

- The Connection Pointe Worldview Website has a series on Jesus' resurrection.
- Video: A ReasonableFaith.org animated video that discusses evidence for three of the historical facts we discussed in this conversation.
- Video: A ReasonableFaith.org animated video that addresses why Jesus' resurrection is the best explanation of key historical facts that are known about Jesus.

If it's really true that Jesus rose from the dead, what does this mean for my life?

1 How would *you* answer the question, "If it's really true that Jesus rose from the dead, what does this mean for my life?"

Here's the answer we'll explore:

"Jesus' resurrection confirms his divine authority and teachings, proving that death is defeated and you have the opportunity for forgiveness of sins and eternal life through faith in him. It means Christianity is true, and you should believe it. You should also live for Jesus and share this good news with others."

2 Now, let's walk through this answer . . .

*Part 1: "**Jesus' resurrection <u>confirms</u> his divine <u>authority</u> and teachings . . .**"*

Imagine that your very skinny friend tells you, "I just won the school's bench press competition. I lifted 450 pounds!" Now, that sounds impressive. But without some good evidence that he did this, it's probably fair for you to be skeptical.

Obviously, anyone can make big claims. Anyone can say they're a superhero or that they're the greatest at something. In fact, anyone can claim to be God—and plenty of crazy people have done just that. But unless there's evidence to back it up, those claims don't hold much weight.

But here's the thing about Jesus: When he claimed to be God (John 5:18; John 8:58; John 10:30) and said he could forgive our sins (Matthew 9:6; Mark 2:5–7; Luke 5:20–24), he didn't just say it. He backed it up. And the resurrection was the ultimate proof.

Jesus' resurrection was God's way of publicly declaring to the world, "Jesus is not guilty of the blasphemy that the Jewish leaders accused him of" (see Matthew 26:63–65). Blasphemy, in this case, means claiming to be on the same level as God, which Jesus did when he said he was God and could forgive sins. But here's the important part: it wasn't just some random guy who came back to life—it was Jesus, the same person who had made those unbelievable claims. So, when God raised him from the dead, he was telling us that Jesus' claims are not crazy. They're actually true!

Q. Why do you think Jesus didn't just claim to be God without any evidence? How does the fact that God made a "public statement" by raising Jesus change the way you view the Bible and Christianity as a whole?

Part 2: "Jesus' resurrection <u>confirms</u> his divine <u>authority</u> and teachings, proving that <u>death</u> is defeated . . ."

Not only does the resurrection prove Jesus' identity and teachings, but it also proves that there is life after death and hope beyond the grave. Death, our ultimate enemy, will not have the last word.

Death is something many people try not to think about. It's a reminder that, no matter how much we achieve or how much we care, everything in this world seems temporary. The relationships you treasure, the things you hold dear, your status and identity, your entire life—everything seems to vanish when you die. It can be terrifying to think that death is the final chapter of your story.

But the resurrection of Jesus changes everything about how we view death! Instead of seeing death as the end of everything we love, Jesus' resurrection proves that death is merely a transition to a new life. The resurrection is not just an amazing display of God's power; it is the proof that death isn't the end. We can know that there is life beyond the grave because Jesus left his grave. It means that this life is part of a larger, ongoing story.

This good news is why the apostle Paul taunts death in 1 Corinthians 15:55–57, saying, "O death, where is your victory? O death, where is your sting? The sting of death is sin, and the power of sin is the law. But thanks be to God, who gives us the victory through our Lord Jesus Christ." Paul is celebrating the victory that Jesus' resurrection gives us—victory over death itself and a new hope and purpose that doesn't end with the grave.

Q. How does Jesus' resurrection change the way you view death and the meaning and purpose of your life? How can the hope of life after death impact the way you live your life today?

*Part 3: "Jesus' resurrection <u>confirms</u> his divine <u>authority</u> and teachings, proving that <u>death</u> is defeated **and you have the opportunity for <u>forgiveness</u> of sins and eternal life through <u>faith</u> in him . . ."***

Jesus' resurrection doesn't just mean that we will rise from the dead and have some kind of life beyond the grave; it means that we are being offered a *perfect* life—an eternity in a perfect place in the presence of a loving God!

The resurrection proves that God loves you more than you could ever truly grasp—enough for him to suffer deeply for you. We all deserve death for our sins (Romans 6:23), but the resurrection confirms that Jesus truly took that punishment on the cross (1 Peter 2:24). We have clear evidence that God's grace is available to us, and that we can live forever with him in a place of unending love and goodness (Revelation 21:3–4). It's more than just a promise—it's a guarantee. God didn't just make a way for us; he came into our world and suffered with us and for us.

Because of the resurrection, we need not fear the future. We can trust Jesus when he claims to be "the way, the truth, and the life"—the only way to salvation (John 14:6). When we accept his sacrifice by grace through faith (Ephesians 2:8–9), we no longer have to worry about whether we're "good enough" to be saved. The resurrection reminds us that we don't have to measure up on our own—Jesus measured up for us. And because of that, we can know that we are saved (1 John 5:13).

Q. Jesus' resurrection demonstrates that you are offered an eternity in a perfect place with a loving God—and that Jesus earned this for you. What does this mean to you personally?

Part 4: "Jesus' resurrection <u>confirms</u> his divine <u>authority</u> and teachings, proving that <u>death</u> is defeated and you have the opportunity for <u>forgiveness</u> of sins and eternal life through <u>faith</u> in him. **It means Christianity is <u>true</u>, and you should believe it** . . ."

The resurrection also means that the truth of Christianity is firmly anchored in history. To become a Christian, you aren't asked to believe in a religious leader's philosophical ideas or spiritual concepts with no evidence. Instead, Christianity's core claim is based on a specific event in history—an event that can be investigated and is supported by multiple well-established historical facts, as we've already seen.

If you believe there is good reason to think that God exists (as discussed in the first section of this book) and that Jesus rose from the dead (as we've explored in the previous chapter), then it follows that you should believe in the Christian God. You should believe that Jesus is who he claimed to be, and that Christianity is, in fact, true. While you may still have questions or areas to explore, the resurrection stands at the center of the Christian faith. If Jesus truly resurrected, then Christianity isn't just another belief system—it is the truth that changes everything.

Q. What would you say to someone who believes that Christianity is just about following the random teachings of ancient people, and there's no way to investigate whether it is actually true?

*Part 5: "Jesus' resurrection <u>confirms</u> his divine <u>authority</u> and teachings, proving that <u>death</u> is defeated and you have the opportunity for <u>forgiveness</u> of sins and eternal life through <u>faith</u> in him. It means Christianity is <u>true</u>, and you should believe it. **You should also live for Jesus and <u>share</u> this good news with others.**"*

Not only should you believe that Christianity is true if Jesus rose from the dead, but you also need to place your faith in him and *commit* your life to him. It's one thing to believe something is true, but it's another to fully embrace it and act on it. For instance, you might believe that a dating relationship is unhealthy and that it's time to move on, but emotionally, it's hard to take that step. Or, you might know that exercising regularly is important for your health, but you don't follow through on it.

In the same way, it's possible to believe that Jesus resurrected to prove he died for your sins, but still be hesitant to commit your life to him and accept his gift. Why would you do that? Why reject the most incredible gift ever offered—the chance to be forgiven for everything you've done wrong and to experience eternal happiness and love in God's presence? Why miss out on the incredible life God wants to give you?

The resurrection of Jesus isn't just a fact to believe—it's an invitation to receive a gift that can change everything. You should believe in this gift and accept it today. Then, share the good news with others. We all have the deadly condition of sin, and we all need the cure—Jesus. If you believe in the resurrection, don't wait—accept God's offer now, live for him, and help others find this same hope.

Q. Why might someone believe in the truth of Christianity but still hesitate to commit their life to Jesus? If you believe Christianity is true, are there areas where you aren't living it out?

3 Can you fill in the blanks from memory?

If it's really true that Jesus rose from the dead, what does this mean for my life?

"Jesus' resurrection c____ (*confirms*) his divine a____ (*authority*) and teachings, proving that d____ (*death*) is defeated and you have the opportunity for f____ (*forgiveness*) of sins and eternal life through f__ (*faith*) in him. It means Christianity is t____ (*true*), and you should believe it. You should also live for Jesus and s____ (*share*) this good news with others."

4 Continuing the Conversation . . .

Knowing: Drawing upon what you learned in this conversation, write down 3–5 ways Jesus' resurrection impacts (or should impact) your own life. Aim to be specific.

Doing: Read these Bible passages: Romans 6:1–14; 2 Corinthians 5:14–21; and Philippians 3:8–11. Reflect on how Jesus' sacrifice for you should lead you to show your love for God and others. Write down one specific thing you will commit to doing this week because Jesus died for you. It should be something that you are not already doing, and it should be a way to demonstrate your love for God or others.

Sharing: Share with a friend or family member how Jesus' resurrection affects your life. Perhaps explain how it gives you hope beyond death, motivates you to forgive others, encourages you when you are suffering, or whatever else is on your heart.

5 Additional Resources

Scriptures & Print Resources:
- Scriptures: Matthew 26:57–68; Luke 5:17–26; John 3:16; John 5:18; John 8:58; John 11:17–27; John 14:6; Romans 6:1–23; 1 Corinthians 15:50–58; 2 Corinthians

5:14–21; Ephesians 2:8–10; Philippians 3:8–11; 1 Thessalonians 4:13–18; 1 Peter 1:3–12; 1 Peter 2:24; Revelation 21:1–4

- Book: Gary R. Habermas, *The Risen Jesus and Future Hope.* Lanham, MD: Rowman & Littlefield, 2003. Chapters 5–10 emphasize important implications that Jesus' resurrection has for our lives.

Online Resources:

Note: To link to these resources, click the QR code below or go to www.Renew.org/GC

- The Connection Pointe Worldview Website has a series that discusses how the resurrection shapes our identity and changes our lives.
- Video: William Lane Craig offers five applications of Jesus' resurrection for our lives.
- Article: Daniel McCoy, "What Is the Meaning of Easter?" This article uses *EASTER* as an acronym to walk through the implications of Jesus' resurrection for our lives.
- Brief Online Article: The "Got Questions" website discusses the importance of Jesus' resurrection.

PRIVACY.FLOWCODE.COM

How does Jesus' death save me from my sins?

1 How would *you* answer the question, "How does Jesus' death save me from my sins?"

Here's the answer we'll explore:

> "Jesus became like us so that we can become like him. Though perfect, he became human, died in our place, and was raised from death to life. When we place our faith in Jesus, our old self dies and we are raised to a new life, in which we are saved from sin's penalty, power, and, one day, even its presence."

2 Now, let's walk through this answer.

Part 1: "Jesus became like <u>us</u> so that we can become like <u>him</u>..."

Have you read any of the "bad plot summaries" that are going around the internet? For example, here's a bad plot summary of the *Lord of the Rings* movies: "Group spends nine hours returning jewelry." Here's one for *Star Wars: The Empire Strikes Back*: "Talking frog convinces son to kill his dad." And here's one for Shrek: "A guy learns to love a girl without her Instagram filters."

Sometimes people do the same thing with Christianity. They try to sum it up in a way that sounds like a bad plot summary. They might say something like, "The point of Christianity is that God hates sin and punishes people because of it." But that summary totally misses God's grace! Or how about this: "The point of Christianity is to get along and be nice to people." But that summary totally leaves God out of the picture!

And yet here's a one-sentence summary that's actually pretty helpful: "The Christian story is that Jesus became like us so that we can become like him." Now, sure, there's a lot more to the story. But this summary gets at the heart of what God did throughout the Bible and why he did it.

First, Jesus is God, but he became a man. Although divine, he added a human nature and became like us. The Gospel of John calls Jesus the "Word," and says, "The Word became flesh and made his dwelling among us" (John 1:14a). Philippians 2 says that Jesus "being in very nature God . . . humbled himself by becoming obedient to death—even death on a cross!" (Philippians 2:6a, 8b).

And why did Jesus become like us? It was so that we could become like him. In later parts of this conversation, we'll describe more about *how* Jesus makes us like him. But for now, consider these scriptures that talk about God transforming us to be like Jesus. Second Corinthians 3:18a says that "we all . . . are being transformed into his image with ever-increasing glory." Romans 8:29 says that God has planned for us to be "conformed to the image of his Son." First John 3:2b promises those who have placed their faith in Jesus that, "when Christ appears, we shall be like him."

So again, Jesus became like us so that we can become like him.

Q. Think about Jesus' life and death. What are some real-life struggles or experiences Jesus went through that show he truly became like us?

Part 2: "Jesus became like us so that we can become like him. **Though perfect, he became human, died in our place. . ."**

Why couldn't God just forgive us for sins? Why would Jesus need to die in our place? Isn't that harsh and unnecessary?

If you've ever started reading the Bible from the beginning, you might notice a pattern: when somebody chooses to do something wrong, everything feels tense and messed up until things are made right. For example, when Adam and Eve, the first two humans, deliberately eat from the one tree God told them not to, things get tense. They become anxious and embarrassed and start blaming each other—until God comes and gives them their punishment. That punishment was that they would have to leave the paradise he created for them and live in a harsher world where they will eventually die.

Then, in the very next generation, there's a murder in the family. One brother kills the other, and God comes and tells the murderer, "What have you done? Listen! Your brother's blood cries out to me from the ground" (Genesis 4:10). Something has again gone wrong with the world, and it won't be made right until the sin is paid for.

This pattern keeps repeating. Just a few chapters later, all the people have become so violent toward each other that God grieves that he made them. So God plans to flood the earth and start over. Again, the message is clear: when somebody chooses to do something wrong, there's a problem; there's a tension hanging in the air until things are made right. The need for justice never goes away until the penalty is paid.

That's why, when God establishes a nation built on his laws, called Israel, he puts in place a system of punishments for dealing with sin: animal sacrifices. If someone sinned, they had to offer an animal—one without flaws—as a substitute. So, if you had committed a significant sin and needed to offer an animal from your flock to God, you were learning some important lessons. For example,

- God takes sin seriously.
- Sin always costs something.
- Sin takes something good and innocent and destroys it.
- God wants to provide something that takes your place so that you aren't the one paying the ultimate penalty for your sin.

But did animal sacrifices actually remove peoples' sins? No, the animal sacrifices were more like cleaning your room by shoving everything under the bed—maybe it looks clean for a bit, but the mess is still there, and it keeps spilling back out. Humanity needed something better—something more permanent to pay our sin penalty.

So, if you keep reading through the Old Testament, you'll come to the writings of Isaiah, a prophet God used to give important messages to the people. In one of these prophetic messages, God showed Isaiah how, sometime in the future, a person (not an animal) would die for the sins of the people. *He* would be the substitute who would pay the penalty for all the people. Isaiah 53:5–6 says,

> "But he was pierced for our transgressions, he was crushed for our iniquities; the punishment that brought us peace was on him, and by his wounds we are healed. We all, like sheep, have gone astray, each of us has turned to our own way; and the LORD has laid on him the iniquity of us all."

Whom was Isaiah was writing about? Jesus—the Messiah. Jesus, though fully God, became human. He lived a perfect life but willingly died in our place. He took the penalty for our sins so that we wouldn't have to pay it. Instead of ignoring our sins (which no just judge would do), God dealt with them himself. Since God is *both* just and loving, the way to rescue us was for Jesus, the God-man, to take our penalty. Because he was sinless and deserved no punishment, Jesus could choose to take the penalty that we deserve.

Q. In your own words, how would you answer if someone asked you why God couldn't just forgive us for our sins, without going to all the trouble to send Jesus?

*Part 3: "Jesus became like us so that we can become like him. Though perfect, he became human, died in our place, **and was raised from death to life.** When we place our faith in Jesus, our old self dies . . ."*

Crucifixion was the Roman Empire's way of saying "game over." You lost. And when Jesus was crucified, it looked like the end of the movement he had started. But then Jesus didn't stay dead. He rose again and appeared to his followers, proving that he was alive. That changed everything. It made us look back on his death and realize it wasn't just a tragic end to his life–it was his plan all along. He chose to die as the final, once-and-for-all sacrifice to take the penalty for our sins upon himself. Just like animal sacrifices were meant to deal with sin, Jesus' death did that permanently. Hebrews 10:10 puts it this way, "We have been made holy through the sacrifice of the body of Jesus Christ once for all."

And did you know that Jesus' death and resurrection are meant to be a picture of what happens to us too? When we place our faith in Jesus, we go through a death-and-resurrection of our own. That's what baptism is all about. Romans 6:3–4 says:

"Or don't you know that all of us who were baptized into Christ Jesus were baptized into his death? We were therefore buried with him through baptism into death in order that, just as Christ was raised from the dead through the glory of the Father, we too may live a new life. For if we have been united with him in a death like his, we will certainly also be united with him in a resurrection like his. For we know that our old self was crucified with him so that the body ruled by sin might be done away with that we should no longer be slaves to sin."

Jesus became like us so that we can become like him. His death and resurrection are facts in history, but they're also more than that. They are also an invitation for you to start a brand-new life right now!

Q. Throughout the Bible, why do you think Jesus' death and resurrection are brought up again and again in sermons and writings? How can you keep reminding yourself again and again of Jesus' death and resurrection?

*Part 4: "Jesus became like us so that we can become like him. Though perfect, he became human, died in our place, and was raised from death to life. When we place our faith in Jesus, our old self dies **and we are raised to a new life, in which we are saved** . . ."*

Let's say you've made it a habit of speeding and driving your car recklessly, and eventually you are pulled over and the authorities take away your driver's license. So you visit your local DMV to figure out how to get it back. You find out it's a huge process involving fees, a suspension period, driving classes, and a ton of paperwork. But, finally, your driver's license is reinstated. What should you do next?

Well, obviously, you'll want to take the shiny new plastic card and frame it on the wall, right? Maybe take some selfies with the driver's license in the background and post it on social media? Maybe invite some friends to come celebrate? But after all that, let's say you never actually take it off the wall and slide the license into your wallet. You never drive around with it. In fact, you never get around to driving again. But at least you've got the license, right?

Now, that would be rather pointless. What is the actual point of having your license reinstated? It's so that you can drive again! In the same way, what is the actual point of having your sins paid for and forgiven? What are you supposed to do now that Jesus has taken your sins away? For what purpose has your old self died?

The whole point is that you are raised to live a *new* life. In this new life, you are no longer a slave to sin; instead, you are empowered to live a life of love, joy, and peace–a life empowered by your faith in Jesus. As Galatians 2:20 describes it, "I have been crucified with Christ and I no longer live, but Christ lives in me. The life I now live in the body, I live by faith in the Son of God, who loved me and gave himself for me."

In other words, you were set free so you could really live. Don't just hang grace on the wall. Live out your new life.

Q. Paul says, "I live by faith in the Son of God." What are some ways you can tell that you are living by faith in Jesus?

Part 5: "Jesus became like us so that we can become like him. Though perfect, he became human, died in our place, and was raised from death to life. When we place our faith in Jesus, our old self dies and we are raised to a new life, in which we are saved **from sin's penalty, power, and, one day, even its presence."**

A helpful way to describe how Jesus saves us is a 3-step process, with each step starting with *P*. First, God saves us from the *penalty* of sin. This is what the Bible often calls "justification." It happens when you place your faith in Jesus and become a Christian. Your sins are forgiven and you're made right with God. This is what Peter was talking about when the Church began:

> Peter replied, "Repent and be baptized, every one of you, in the name of Jesus Christ for the forgiveness of your sins. And you will receive the gift of the Holy Spirit." (Acts 2:38)

Second, God saves us from the *power* of sin. This isn't just a one-time event; it's a process which the Bible sometimes calls "sanctification." From the moment you first become a Christian until the moment you die, the Holy Spirit lives and works within you to make you more like Jesus. The result? Sin has less and less of a grip on you; it doesn't control you like it used to. After listing many important sins that once defined his audience (sexual immorality, greed, theft, etc.), Paul explains this good news:

> "And that is what some of you were. But you were washed, you were sanctified, you were justified in the name of the Lord Jesus Christ and by the Spirit of our God." (1 Corinthians 6:11)

Third, God will one day save us from the very *presence* of sin. This is something we'll experience in the future, in heaven. In eternity, sin won't even be appealing. It will feel as tempting as eating used gauze out of a dumpster. Why? Because sin only thrives when we don't have joy, and we will have complete joy in God's presence: "You will fill me with joy in your presence, with eternal pleasures at your right hand" (Psalm 16:11). The Bible describes this condition of finally being free from the very presence of sin as "glorifying" us or "glorification" (see Romans 8:30).

So here's the big picture: Christians have been saved (from sin's penalty), are being saved (from its power), and will be saved (from its presence). And at every step, it's all through faith in Jesus Christ.

Q. Can you explain the three steps of God saving us?

3 Can you fill in the blanks from memory?

How does Jesus' death save me from my sins?

"Jesus became like u____ (*us*) so that we can become like h___ (*him*). Though p___ (*perfect*), he became h___ (*human*), died in our p___ (*place*), and was raised from death to l___ (*life*). When we place our f___ (*faith*) in Jesus, our old self d___ (*dies*) and we are raised to a new l___ (*life*), in which we are s___ (*saved*) from sin's p___ (*penalty*), p___ (*power*), and, one day, even its p___ (*presence*)."

4 Continuing the Conversation . . .

Knowing: Read 2 Corinthians 5:21. After reading this verse a few times, can you try to recite it from memory?

Doing: Pray through the three steps of salvation, thanking God for what he has done, is doing, and will do in your life.

Sharing: Ask somebody if they know how Jesus' death saves us from their sins. If they could use some help with their answer, offer them some of the scriptures and truths you learned from this conversation. It might be especially helpful to describe the three steps of salvation discussed in the final part of this conversation.

5 Additional Resources

Scriptures & Print Resources:

- Scriptures: John 1:1–3, 14; Philippians 2:5–11; Hebrews 10:11–14; 1 Corinthians 6:9–11; 2 Corinthians 5:21; Galatians 2:20; Romans 6:3–4
- Book: Matthew W. Bates, *The Gospel Precisely: Surprisingly Good News About Jesus Christ the King*. Renew.org, 2021. This short book walks through what the gospel is, why we need it, and the ways we benefit from it.

Online Resources:

Note: To link to these resources, click the QR code below or go to www.Renew.org/GC

- Article: John Whittaker, "How Did Jesus Die for Our Sins?" This article walks through biblical concepts such as Passover and the Day of Atonement to show the sacrificial nature of Jesus' death for us.
- Article: Jim Frech, "Salvation: We Have Been, Are Being, and Shall Be Saved." This article discusses three crucial facets of salvation for those who place faith in Jesus.
- Article: Nathan Guy, "Come to the Water: Accepting Christ's Invitation to Baptism." This article explores the beauty of baptism and various ways it identifies us with Christ.
- The Connection Pointe Worldview Website has a series that addresses the significance of Jesus dying for our sins and the concept of salvation by grace through faith.

People in other religions claim to have experienced God. Do they have the Holy Spirit too?

1 **How would *you* answer the question, "People in other religions claim to have experienced God. Do they have the Holy Spirit too?"**

Here's the answer we'll explore:

> "Although other religions can help people make it through life and have meaningful experiences, not all spirits are from God, and only one religion can be the true one. The Holy Spirit moves us toward Jesus and makes us more like him."

2 Now, let's walk through this answer.

Part 1: "Although other religions can help people make it through life and have meaningful experiences . . ."

What exactly is a religion? Can you try to give a definition? There are a lot of religions out there, with Christianity, Islam, Buddhism, and Hinduism being the largest ones. Each religion differs from the next in all sorts of ways. So is there a good definition of religion that fits *all* the religions? World religions expert Winfried Corduan helps us here by explaining that every religion is a system of beliefs and practices that points a person toward something beyond this world–something "out there" (what's sometimes called *transcendence*). And thus, each religion offers a person a way to find meaning and make sense of life.[17] That's a helpful definition.

Did you catch what makes up a religion? It's things like beliefs, practices, and a connection to something beyond ourselves, and these sorts of things help a person find meaning and make sense of life. Now, it's totally possible for a religion to have all those things and still get its answers completely wrong. Even if a religion isn't true, it can still give people some helpful ways to get through life. With the answers it gives, it helps people make sense of the world. It'll usually give moral dos and don'ts (guidance on what it takes to be a good, wise person). It often has a community of people who support each other. And it shows people how to connect with its version of God, or whatever it teaches is "out there" beyond us. Again, that doesn't mean all the religions are *true*. It just means each religion helps people make it through life in its own way.

Now, for some people, just getting through life is all that really matters to them. They're not all that concerned about discovering what's actually *true* or what comes in the *next* life. For them, it's mainly just about getting through *this* life and being as happy as possible. And religions help with that by giving people a sense of purpose and community. So, if you think the only real point of life is just getting through it, you'll probably start thinking that it doesn't really matter what religion you follow, as long as it works for you. However, if you really do care about truth, you'll take the next step and explore which religion is actually true.

Q. Can you remember the main parts of Winfried Corduan's definition of religion? It would be good to be able to commit them to memory. *(According to Corduan, every religion is a system of beliefs and practices which direct a person toward some kind of transcendence (something that exists "out there.")*

Part 2: "Although other religions can help people make it through life and have meaningful experiences, not all spirits are from God . . ."

Let's tell three stories, all three involving angels who are said to have taught about Jesus. For the sake of space, we'll tell the short version of these stories.

Story A. A man and woman were engaged to be married when an angel appeared to each of them separately. The angel explained that the woman was going to become pregnant with a child from heaven. The Holy Spirit would come upon her and she would become pregnant and give birth to a divine child. Because this divine human would be "God with us," he would be called the "Son of God."

Story B. An angel approached a middle-aged man and told him that he would be God's chosen messenger to teach the world how to submit to God. Whenever the angel gave him a message, the man would recite it and teach it to others. In these messages from the angel, one person was mentioned over ninety times: Jesus. But the angel explained that Jesus was not the Son of God, because it would be impossible for God to become a human. Instead, Jesus was an exalted prophet.

Story C. A young man was wondering which church he should join, when an angel appeared and told him that all of them were corrupt. That led to a series of visits from the angel, who gave the young man messages from God over several years. According to the angel, Jesus was the Son of God—but also the first of many children born to God. As it turns out, God was once a human, but he progressed to become God. And we are all children of God and his wife. If we follow the angel's messages, we too can become gods.

Do you know which religion each of these stories comes from? Story A is from Christianity. Story B is from Islam. Story C is from the Church of Jesus Christ of Latter-Day Saints (sometimes called Mormonism).

All three stories tell of an angel coming and giving a message about Jesus; but they can't all be right because the three angels contradicted each other. That means at least two of them had to be telling lies. That's a big deal. It shows that just because someone claims to have a spiritual experience, that doesn't mean the experience is really from the one true God. Other religions can offer life advice or meaningful experiences, but not all spirits are from God. As the Bible warns, "Test the spirits to see whether they are from God" (1 John 4:1).

Q. Read Galatians 1:8–9. What is it that Paul is warning his readers about?

*Part 3: "Although other <u>religions</u> can help people make it through <u>life</u> and have meaningful <u>experiences</u>, not all spirits are from <u>God</u>, **and only one religion can be the <u>true</u> one**. . ."*

Before we keep going, let's circle back to something we said earlier. A lot of people care only about what helps them get through *this* life. They're not thinking about the *next* life. They're not all that concerned with what's true and false; they mainly want what's going to help them cope in this life. So, for them, it doesn't really matter which religion someone follows, or if you follow a particular religion at all, as long as it helps them right now. But that's a very different question from asking, *"What's actually true?"* If we care about what's actually true, we've got to think more carefully.

When we look at all the major religions out there, it can feel intimidating. There are so many, and billions of people follow them. It can be easy to hope that, maybe, somehow they're all true. Is it possible that, in the end, all the religions are true? Maybe they all save people in their own way? That might sound comforting because then we wouldn't have to worry about picking the wrong one. But there's a problem with that idea.

The reality is, the world's religions contradict each other in all sorts of ways. For example, Christianity says that Jesus is God, while Islam says Jesus is most definitely not God. They can't both be right. Christianity and Islam both teach that God created the world; but Buddhism teaches that, instead of being created by a purposeful God, the world came about through an unfortunate chain of cause-and-effect conditions. That's a major difference.

And what about reincarnation? Buddhism and Hinduism both teach that people are reborn again and again based on karma (how they lived past lives). But even though they both believe in reincarnation, they offer very different solutions on how to end this repeating cycle of rebirths. For example, many Hindus say the goal is to be united with a Supreme Being, whereas Buddhism says the goal is to release all attachments and enter the "extinguishing" of nirvana.

Even their ideas about God are different. Hinduism has many gods, and they are very different from the one God of Islam (Allah). Likewise, Allah differs in character from the God of Christianity. These views of God simply don't match.

And that's just a few examples of differences between four of the biggest religions. There are dozens more religions, and they all contradict each other in many ways. If we really care about truth, we can't pretend they're all saying the same thing or they're all true. Believing that all religions are true means we have to believe thousands of contradictions are true all at once. If we're being logical, that doesn't make sense. We have to admit that there can only be one true religion.

Q. Pick a non-Christian religion that you know about. What is a major similarity this religion has with Christianity? What is a major difference?

Part 4: "Although other religions can help people make it through life and have meaningful experiences, not all spirits are from God, and only one religion can be the true one. **The Holy Spirit moves us toward Jesus** *. . ."*

Not every spirit is from God, and not every spiritual experience is with God. When the Bible talks about the *Holy* Spirit, it doesn't describe just a general "spiritual force." The Holy Spirit doesn't just move us toward religion in general or spiritual experiences in general. Rather, we see a Spirit who has a very specific mission—moving us toward Jesus.

Jesus promised his disciples that, after he left the earth, he would send someone in his place, the Holy Spirit. And what would the Holy Spirit do all over the world? In John 15:26, Jesus said, "When the Advocate comes, whom I will send to you from the Father—the Spirit of truth who goes out from the Father—he will testify about me." Did you catch that? Jesus said the Holy Spirit would testify about him—that is, he would help to convince people to know, trust, and follow Jesus.

The Holy Spirit also gives Jesus' followers the power to tell others about Jesus. In Acts 1:8, Jesus promises his disciples: "But you will receive power when the Holy Spirit comes on you; and you will be my witnesses in Jerusalem, and in all Judea and Samaria, and to the ends of the earth."

So again, not every spirit is from God. Some spiritual influences actually lead people away from Jesus. That's why 1 John 4:1 warns us, "Dear friends, do not believe every spirit, but test the spirits to see whether they are from God, because many false prophets have gone out into the world."

But here's the good news: if you are truly following the Holy Spirit's lead and not resisting him, he will always lead you right to Jesus. And that's where you'll find the forgiveness, truth, righteousness, peace, and purpose that you were made for and long for.

Q. Read 1 John 4:1–3. According to this passage, how can we tell if a spiritual message is from God?

Part 5: "Although other religions can help people make it through life and have meaningful experiences, not all spirits are from God, and only one religion can be the true one. The Holy Spirit moves us toward Jesus and makes us more like him."

What do the lonely boy at summer camp, the spouse away at war, the kindergartner crying on her first day of school, and the gloomy freshman at college all have in common? They all miss *home.*

But what is it about home that makes people miss it so much? People miss the goodnight hugs, the favorite meals on birthdays, the celebrations after graduation, the "I love you's" before bed, and the "Good jobs" after winning the big game. That's called love. What can make home such a great place? It's when it's a place filled with love.

People also miss the inside jokes, the favorite board games, the silly Christmas traditions, the ridiculous home videos, and the moments of laughter. Another word for that is *joy.* Home feels special when it's a place of joy.

And people also miss the Sunday afternoon naps, the calm rest after a hard day at school or work, the lazy lull after dinner, the shoulder to cry on, and the barbecue in the yard. Another word for that is *peace.* Home feels safe and restful when it's a place of *peace.*

So what makes home so special? It's the love, joy, and peace.

And here's something amazing: those are the first three items in a list called the "fruit of the Spirit." These are three qualities that the Holy Spirit grows (like fruit) in the lives of disciples of Jesus. In the book of Galatians, the apostle Paul first lists what he calls the "acts of the flesh"—things we naturally do when we're following our sinful desires. These are things like sexual impurity, idolatry, hatred, jealousy, fits of rage, selfish ambition, and drunkenness. They might seem fun at first, but they lead to chaos and destruction. Then, Paul follows this up by listing the kinds of things the Holy Spirit will grow in our lives as we live lives of faith in Jesus. He writes, "But the fruit of the Spirit is love, joy, peace, forbearance, kindness, goodness, faithfulness, gentleness and self-control" (Galatians 5:22–23a). If you're letting the Holy Spirit grow these qualities in your life, then you're becoming more like Jesus, because he's the one who lived all these perfectly.

That's exactly what the Holy Spirit wants to do in your life: make you like Jesus. But here's the key thing: you don't get the "fruit of the Spirit" by trying really hard to produce the fruit. Trees don't produce fruit by effort; they have to be connected to water and sunlight. In the same way, we can't produce love, joy, peace, and other fruit on our own. We have to be connected to the Holy Spirit.

How do we do that? It happens as we stop being the boss of our life and doing what comes naturally to us; instead, we start letting the Holy Spirit lead us. We learn Scripture, and when the Holy Spirit reminds us of Scripture we've learned, we listen. The more we let him lead us, the more we become like Jesus—full of love, joy, peace, and so much more.

Q. Read Galatians 5:22-23a. Can you repeat the "fruit of the Spirit" from memory? What is one way that you want the Holy Spirit to help you become more like Jesus?

3 Can you fill in the blanks from memory?

People in other religions claim to have experienced God. Do they have the Holy Spirit too?

"Although other r___ (*religions*) can help people make it through l___ (*life*) and have meaningful e___ (*experiences*), not all spirits are from G___ (*God*), and only one religion can be the t___ (*true*) one. The H___ (*Holy*) Spirit moves us toward J___ (*Jesus*) and makes us more like h___ (*him*)."

4 Continuing the Conversation . . .

Knowing: A core truth from this conversation is that Christianity isn't just about helping you make it through this life. Read 1 Corinthians 15:17-19 and think through what Paul is saying.

Doing: Think of someone you know who follows a different religion or different life philosophy from Christianity. Take some time today and pray that the Holy Spirit moves this person toward Jesus.

Sharing: Imagine that someone says to you, "People in other religions claim to have experienced God. Do they have the Holy Spirit too?" In your own words, how might you answer them, using what you learned from this conversation?

5 Additional Resources

Scriptures & Print Resources:

- Scriptures: Galatians 1:8–9; John 15:26; Acts 1:8; 1 John 4:1–3; Galatians 5:22–23.
- Book: David Young, *Holy Spirit: Filled, Empowered, and Led.* Renew.org, 2021. This short book explores who the Holy Spirit is and how he makes us Christlike.
- Book: Daniel J. McCoy, editor, *The Popular Handbook of World Religions.* Eugene, OR: Harvest House Publishers, 2021. This handbook summarizes the world's religions and explores how Christians can connect with adherents of other religions.
- Book: Winfried Corduan, *Neighboring Faiths: A Christian Introduction to World Religions.* Downers Grove: IVP Academic, 2024. This handbook explores each world

religion as it is lived out followed by a practical section called "So you meet a . . . [Buddhist, Hindu, etc.]."

Online Resources:

Note: To link to these resources, click the QR code below or go to www.Renew.org/GC

- Article: Daniel McCoy, "Is Jesus the Only Way?" This article balances the truth that Christians are to live at peace with everybody with the truth that Christianity disagrees with belief systems not grounded in Christ.

- Article: Daniel McCoy, "Are All Religions True?" This article challenges the common idea that if a non-Christian religion seems to help people, it must therefore be true.

- The Connection Pointe Worldview Website has a series that provides an overview and critique of the major world religions.

PRIVACY.FLOWCODE.COM

God's Justice and Goodness

Is the God of the New Testament the same as the God of the Old Testament?

1 How would *you* answer the question, "Is the God of the New Testament the same as the God of the Old Testament?"

Here's the answer we'll explore:

> "The idea that the God of the New Testament (NT) and Old Testament (OT) is different is an ancient heresy. The claim is that God seems judgmental and angry in the OT, but full of love and grace in the NT. Yet the Bible's picture of God is consistent: his love and grace are also seen in the OT, and his anger against sin is also seen in the NT."

2 Now, let's walk through this answer . . .

Part 1: "The idea that the God of the New Testament (NT) and Old Testament (OT) is <u>different</u> is an ancient <u>heresy</u> . . ."

In A.D. 144, a man named Marcion was declared a heretic by Christian church leaders. A "heretic" is someone who holds beliefs that go against core teachings of the Bible—rejecting something that's essential to the Christian faith. And that is exactly what Marcion did. He denied that there is one God who is described throughout the Bible.

Marcion thought that the God of the OT was a different God from the God of the NT. He believed that the OT God was angry, judgmental, quick to punish humans, and inferior to the NT God. By contrast, he saw the NT God as a God of love and grace—the merciful God of Jesus. Marcion disliked the OT God so much that he rejected the OT and didn't consider it part of the Bible.

Marcion's view is a serious error. It goes against what Jesus himself taught. Jesus said there's only one God (Mark 12:29), and he often quoted the OT. He said the OT scriptures will not pass away (Matthew 5:18). Jesus considered the God of the OT to be the one true God—the same God he talked about in the NT (John 8:54–58). In fact, Jesus said that he is the fulfillment of the OT (Matthew 5:17).

So, if Jesus didn't see inconsistency in God in the OT and NT, why did Marcion? Why do some people today still wrestle with thinking God is different in the OT and NT?

Q. Before reading on, why do you think some people see God as angry and judgmental in the OT but loving and merciful in the NT? Also, why is it important that there is one God described throughout all of Scripture?

Part 2: "The idea that the God of the New Testament (NT) and Old Testament (OT) is <u>different</u> is an ancient <u>heresy</u>. **The claim is that God seems judgmental and <u>angry</u> in the OT . . ."**

Let's start by considering why some people see God in the OT as angry, judgmental, and wrathful. This idea comes from the stories where God takes severe action against human evil and rebellion, showing that he takes our sin very seriously. Let's consider a few of these.

One example is the flood in Noah's time (Genesis 6–9). God saw that humanity had become completely corrupt. In response, God decided to bring judgment on the earth by sending a flood, sparing only Noah and his family because they had not fallen into the corruption of the rest of the world.

Another example is the destruction of Sodom and Gomorrah (Genesis 19), cities known for their extreme wickedness. God would have spared the cities if just ten righteous people could be found there (Genesis 18:22–33). However, because the cities had become totally corrupt, God destroyed the cities with fire.

Similarly, when Israel entered the Promised Land, he punished the people who were living in the land (known as the Canaanites). The Canaanites had become incredibly evil, doing horrible things like sacrificing their children to their false gods. So God decided that they must be totally wiped out from the land that he was giving to Israel (Deuteronomy 7, Joshua 6). He warned Israel that they would also be destroyed if they became wicked (Leviticus 18:24–30).

Q. What do these biblical events tell you about how God views our sin? We'll discuss this further as we go; but, at this point, do you think these stories show that God is mean and angry in the OT rather than loving and full of grace? Why or why not?

Part 3: "The idea that the God of the New Testament (NT) and Old Testament (OT) is __different__ is an ancient __heresy__. The claim is that God seems judgmental and __angry__ in the OT, **but full of __love__ and grace in the NT . . .**"

By contrast, some people think God is quite different in the NT—a God who is full of love and grace rather than judgment and wrath. It's certainly true that we see God's love and grace revealed in many ways throughout the NT, especially through the teachings and actions of Jesus.

Many of Jesus' teachings emphasize God's love and grace. An example is the story of the prodigal son (Luke 15:11–32), Jesus illustrates how God, like a loving father, is always ready to forgive us—no matter how far we go astray. In this parable, the father runs to his sinful son and hugs him and forgives him. This represents God's unconditional love and his willingness to forgive even the most sinful.

Jesus also demonstrates God's love and grace through his actions. The famous verse John 3:16 sums this up well when Jesus says: "For God so loved the world that he gave his one and only Son, that whoever believes in him shall not perish but have eternal life." Jesus' death on the cross is the ultimate act of love and grace—though he was innocent, he willingly sacrificed himself for us. He took the punishment we deserve so that we could be forgiven. Jesus constantly healed the sick, stood up for the outcasts, and offered forgiveness to sinners.

Q. Do you think the love and grace we see in Jesus implies that God in the NT is not a judge who takes sin seriously and punishes it strictly? Why or why not?

Part 4: "The idea that the God of the New Testament (NT) and Old Testament (OT) is <u>different</u> is an ancient <u>heresy</u>. The claim is that God seems judgmental and <u>angry</u> in the OT, but full of <u>love</u> and grace in the NT. **Yet the Bible's picture of God is <u>consistent</u>: his love and grace are also seen in the <u>OT</u> . . ."**

But it's important to understand that God is consistent throughout the entire Bible. His character doesn't change. It's not true that God shows no love and grace in the OT, so that all we see is God's punishment of sin. Similarly, it isn't true that God's wrath against sin is absent in the NT, so that only his love and grace are visible. Let's explore the consistent character of God by starting with the OT, where we can see his love and grace shining through, even as he punishes sin.

In the examples of God's judgment from the OT that we discussed earlier, we don't see a bloodthirsty God. Instead, we see a God who longs for people to turn from sin and live. Take the flood, for example. While God sent a flood to destroy humanity, he also gave people time to repent. Noah was a "preacher of righteousness" (2 Peter 2:5), offering people the opportunity to turn from their evil ways before judgment came. Similarly, before destroying Sodom and Gomorrah, God waited until there were not even ten righteous people in the cities (Genesis 18:32), showing he wasn't quick to destroy them but gave them a chance to repent. In the case of the Canaanites, God delayed judgment for over 400 years. They were deeply corrupt, but God cared for them and gave them ample time to repent before their sins reached a point of no return (Genesis 15:13–16).

In all these cases, we see that God's justice is real—sin must be punished because he is a good and just judge. But we also see his love and mercy. God doesn't want anyone to face the consequences of sin. As he says in Ezekiel 33:11, "I take no pleasure in the death of the wicked, but rather that they turn from their ways and live. Turn! Turn from your evil ways!"

In the OT, we often see God's love and compassion for all people. For instance, God sent Jonah to the evil city of Nineveh to warn them that they would be destroyed if they didn't stop sinning. These people were not part of the nation of Israel, but God cared for them—just as he cares for all people. These people didn't "know their right hand from their left" (Jonah 4:11). In other words, they were confused, sinful, and needed to repent. And, after being warned, they repented, and God forgave them.

There are many other examples of God's love and grace in the OT. After God saved Israel from slavery in Egypt, the Israelites constantly disobeyed, yet God showed great patience and didn't destroy them (Exodus 32, Numbers 14). After King David repented of his sins of adultery and murder, God forgave him, though consequences followed (2 Samuel 12). God even had compassion on the evil King Manasseh, who led God's people into horrible sins. When Manasseh repented, God forgave him and allowed him to continue as king (2 Chronicles 33:1–20). Over and over again in the OT, God punishes sin but also offers forgiveness to those who truly repent.

Q. What does Ezekiel 33:11 reveal about God's heart toward you when you sin? Imagine God having great love and grace, yet God refuses to punish sin and injustice and just ignores all wickedness. Would that be a God worthy of worship?

*Part 5: "The idea that the God of the New Testament (NT) and Old Testament (OT) is different is an ancient heresy. The claim is that God seems judgmental and angry in the OT, but full of love and grace in the NT. Yet the Bible's picture of God is consistent: his love and grace are also seen in the OT, **and his anger against sin is also seen in the NT.**"*

Just as God shows love and compassion in the OT, he also demonstrates strict judgment of sin in the NT. Let's look at just a few examples. Consider what happened in Acts 5 to Ananias and Sapphira, who lied to God. God judged them for this sin, and they died as a result. In Acts 12:19–23, we see how God judged King Herod, who was struck down and eaten by worms for his sin. In Acts 13:4–12, God judged Elymas, who opposed God and was struck blind.

Even Jesus—God in the flesh—spoke more about God's judgment and punishment of sin than anyone else in the Bible. He warned often about the dangers of hell, a place of eternal separation from God and punishment for the wicked (e.g., Matthew 5:22; Matthew 10:28; Matthew 25:31–46; Mark 9:43). Jesus shows that God takes sin seriously and won't ignore it.

So, although God is a God of love, grace, and compassion, he clearly does not hesitate to judge sin with severe consequences in the NT. The highest example of God's wrath against sin in the NT is seen in the price Jesus had to pay on the cross for our sins. At the cross, we see God's love in the sacrifice of his Son for our forgiveness. But God's wrath against sin is also made clear—the death of Jesus shows that sin requires severe punishment. This is why Jesus died: to take the wrath of God that we deserve.

Thus, God's qualities are consistent throughout the Bible. In both the OT and NT, God is a God of incredible love and compassion; yet, he's equally a God of justice and righteous wrath against sin.

Q. What does Jesus' sacrifice on the cross tell you about God? Do you see how his love and grace, as well as his justice and punishment of sin, come together at the cross?

3 Can you fill in the blanks from memory?

Is the God of the New Testament the same as the God of the Old Testament?

"The idea that the God of the New Testament (NT) and Old Testament (OT) is d____ (*different*) is an ancient h____ (*heresy*). The claim is that God seems judgmental and a____ (*angry*) in the OT, but full of l____ (*love*) and grace in the NT. Yet the Bible's picture of God is c____ (*consistent*): his love and grace are also seen in the O____ (*OT*), and his anger against sin is also seen in the N____ (*NT*)."

4 Continuing the Conversation . . .

Knowing: Read at least two of these OT passages: 2 Chronicles 33:1–20; Psalm 103:1–14; Isaiah 55:6–7; Ezekiel 33:11. Using what you learned from this entire conversation, explain how these verses show that God is the same in the OT and NT.

Doing: Write down 2–3 reasons why it's a good thing that God punishes sin and does not ignore our evil. Then, write 2–3 reasons why it's a good thing that God wants to forgive us and isn't quick to punish sin. Spend time in prayer, thanking God for his balance of love, grace, and justice. Ask him to help you have these qualities in your own life—being forgiving and loving, while also taking sin seriously.

Sharing: Talk to a friend or family member about what you learned in this conversation. Explain how God's character is consistent across the OT and NT. Perhaps have a role-play conversation where your friend takes the view that God is different in the OT and NT.

5 Additional Resources

Scriptures & Print Resources:

- Scriptures: 2 Chronicles 33:1–20; Psalm 103:1–14; Isaiah 55:6–7; Ezekiel 33:11; Matthew 5:17–18; Matthew 25:31–46; Luke 15:11–32; John 3:16; Romans 5:6–8; 2 Peter 3:9
- Book: Paul Copan, *Is God a Vindictive Bully?: Reconciling Portrayals of God in the Old and New Testaments.* Grand Rapids, MI: Baker Academic, 2022. This book challenges

the claim that the Old Testament God is harsh and unlike Jesus, showing instead that the same God reveals both justice and compassion in both Testaments.

Online Resources:

Note: To link to these resources, click the QR code below or go to www.Renew.org/GC

- Video: Sean McDowell briefly addresses how God is the same throughout the Bible.
- Video: William Lane Craig briefly addresses how God is the same throughout the Bible.

How can I trust a God who has killed people in the Bible?

1 How would *you* answer the question, "How can I trust a God who has killed people in the Bible?"

Here's the answer we'll explore:

> "Sometimes, God's judgment of sin in the Bible involves death. This shows that God takes sin seriously. But he is also full of love and grace, and Jesus proved that. God has the right to give life and take it, but he's never unfair."

2 Now, let's walk through this answer . . .

Part 1: "Sometimes, God's judgment of <u>sin</u> in the Bible involves <u>death</u> . . ."

Let's be honest—some parts of the Bible are hard to read. There are stories where people die suddenly or even where whole groups are wiped out, and it's fair to ask: *How could a loving God do that? Can I really trust him? Does he want to wipe me out too?*

The truth is, there are times in the Bible when God punishes sin with death. For example, in the flood story (Genesis 6–9), God sees that the entire earth is filled with violence and evil, so he sends a flood to start over. Only Noah's family—eight people—are spared because they hadn't completely turned away from God. Then in Genesis 19, God destroys the cities of Sodom and Gomorrah because of their extreme wickedness. In the New Testament, a married couple named Ananias and Sapphira lie to God and fall dead on the spot (Acts 5). And one of the hardest parts of the Bible to process is when God commands the Israelites to drive the wicked Canaanites out of the land that God was giving to Israel. God ordered that no Canaanites be left alive in the land to lead the Israelites into sin (Deuteronomy 20:16–18).

Each of these stories has its own context, and we could spend pages exploring why God acted as he did in each one. But in this brief conversation, we want to focus on a few key truths to help you think about these difficult stories: God is not a bloodthirsty God—he is a God of love and grace who wants every person (including you) to turn from evil. He has the authority to give life and take it, and he always acts with justice. And that's where we'll begin: we worship a God who doesn't ignore sin, and that's actually a very good thing.

Q. What's your honest reaction when you read stories in the Bible about God punishing sin with death? Explain.

Part 2: "Sometimes, God's judgment of <u>sin</u> in the Bible involves <u>death</u>. **This shows God takes sin <u>seriously</u> . . ."**

Imagine if the Bible taught that there's no punishment for evil. No matter what anyone did—lying, cheating, stealing, or even things as terrible as murder, torture, or sexual assault—imagine God would just say, "It's okay, I'm too loving to punish that." Would that actually be a good thing? Would it *really* be loving? Or just? Would you think, "That's a God I want to worship," or would you wonder, "Wait. How could a truly good and fair God let everything slide?"

When we really think about it, we all want a God who stands up for justice. We don't want a world where evil is ignored and wrong goes unpunished. Sin isn't a small thing—it destroys lives, communities, relationships with others, and our relationship with God. A God who never judged sin wouldn't be good or loving. He'd be like a parent who never disciplines his child no matter how badly the child behaves. That kind of God wouldn't be worthy of our worship. He wouldn't even be worthy of being called "God."

So when we read in the Bible that God takes serious action to judge sin, it's actually good news. It means he doesn't ignore evil—he deals with it. He sees every injustice and every wicked deed, and he's not okay with it. He doesn't usually punish sin with immediate physical death, but he does promise that all sin carries the death penalty (Romans 6:23) and must be paid for. That's comforting to know—at least until we realize that God will also deal with the sin and injustice in us.

And that's where some of us start to struggle with trusting God. If God takes sin so seriously, does that mean he's out to get me? Is he just waiting to punish me the moment I mess up? Does he want to squash me, or does he actually want what's best for me? That's the question we'll explore next.

Q. Romans 6:23 says the consequence of sin is death. Does the idea that God takes sin that seriously make you feel nervous, grateful, or something else? Is there a sin in your own life that you ignore and need to take more seriously?

*Part 3: "Sometimes, God's judgment of <u>sin</u> in the Bible involves <u>death</u>. This shows that God takes sin <u>seriously</u>. **But he is also full of love and grace, and <u>Jesus</u> proved that** . . ."*

Even though it's good that God punishes sin, it's easy to read stories of God's judgment and assume that he's harsh or eager to punish us. But nothing could be further from the truth. The Bible paints a much bigger picture of who God is—a God whose love for us is deeper than we can understand (Ephesians 3:17–19) and is not based on how good we are (Romans 5:8). His heart is full of compassion. He doesn't want to bring judgment; he wants to forgive, restore, and rescue us.

Again and again, we see God giving second chances. He sends prophets to warn people and shows mercy when they repent. Think of Jonah and the people of Nineveh (Jonah 3), or how Jesus asked for forgiveness for the very people who crucified him (Luke 23:34). One of the clearest expressions of God's heart is in Ezekiel 33:11: "I take no pleasure in the death of the wicked, but rather that they turn from their ways and live." God's justice is real—but so is his desire to save.

The greatest proof of God's love is Jesus. Instead of leaving us to face the punishment for our sins, God sent his own Son to take our place. Romans 5:8 says that God "demonstrates" or "proves" his love for us by this: "While we were still sinners, Christ died for us" (Romans 5:8). The punishment for sin is death (Romans 6:23), but Jesus—God in human flesh— took that punishment so we could be forgiven. The cross shows us both the seriousness of sin and the depth of God's love. God is both loving and just—and these qualities of God come together at the cross (John 3:16; 2 Corinthians 5:21).

Q. Read Psalm 103:8–14. How might this passage ease your fears that God may not love you or that he may be out to get you? How does Jesus' sacrifice help you understand both God's justice and his love?

Part 4: "Sometimes, God's judgment of <u>sin</u> in the Bible involves <u>death</u>. This shows that God takes sin <u>seriously</u>. But he is also full of love and <u>grace</u>, and <u>Jesus</u> proved that. **God has the <u>right</u> to give life and take it** *. . ."*

We've seen from the Bible that God loves us deeply, and yet his justice means sin must be punished—and the penalty for sin is death. But that raises a tough question: If God is good and loving, how can he bring about the death of so many people, like in the flood or the destruction of Sodom? If it would be wrong for me to wipe out a bunch of people like that, how can it be right for God?

This is where we have to remember something important: we are not God. The Bible makes it clear that God alone gives us life—he created each person, and he keeps us alive with every breath (Acts 17:25). Because he is the Creator, he has the authority over when a life begins and ends (1 Samuel 2:6). We don't have that right, which is why "playing God" is wrong for us. But God is not "playing." He is God, which means he acts with perfect knowledge, justice, goodness, love, and eternal perspective. He chooses how much time we have with the life he gives, and he never does that recklessly.

Job, after losing everything, said, "The Lord gave, and the Lord has taken away; blessed be the name of the Lord" (Job 1:21). Job realized that God has the right to give life and take it away, and we can trust his decisions. Plus, we must remember that death is not the end. According to the Bible, physical death is really just a doorway into eternity—either with God or separated from him (Hebrews 9:27; Matthew 25:46). Only God has the right to decide how long we will live in this world before he moves us on to the next. If I decide that I feel like ending someone's earthly life, I've gone beyond my authority. And, as we'll see next, we can trust that God is fair in making decisions about life and death.

Q. Why is it different when God decides how long someone lives, compared to when humans try to "play God" and take that authority into their own hands? What makes it hard to trust God's decisions about life and death?

*Part 5: "Sometimes, God's judgment of <u>sin</u> in the Bible involves <u>death</u>. This shows God takes sin <u>seriously</u>. But he is also full of love and <u>grace</u>, and <u>Jesus</u> proved that. God has the <u>right</u> to give life and take it, **but he's never unfair.**"*

Here's one more truth to hold on to: God is never unfair. That might be hard to believe when we see injustices in this world and read difficult stories in the Bible. But Scripture is clear: God is the perfect Judge. Unlike a human judge who has limited knowledge and goodness and can make mistakes, God always judges correctly.

This was something Abraham discovered when talking to God about God's plans to destroy Sodom. "The Judge of all the earth" will do what is right (Genesis 18:25). God knows all the consequences of every action, understands why we do what we do, and never misunderstands us or fails to love us. He sees the whole picture—including eternity. So, his justice and decisions are perfect, even when they are beyond our understanding.

As Psalm 145:17 says, "The Lord is righteous in all his ways and faithful in all he does." And Jesus is the ultimate proof of God's goodness and love. Through his death and resurrection—real events supported by strong historical evidence (see *Conversation 9*)— Jesus showed us that God is not distant or uncaring. He is faithful, compassionate, and always looking out for our good.

So even when we don't understand his ways, we can trust that God is never unfair. He always does what is right.

Q. Have you ever felt like God's actions in the Bible seemed unfair? What made it feel that way? How can you remind yourself of God's justice and goodness?

3 Can you fill in the blanks from memory?

How can I trust a God who has killed people in the Bible?

"Sometimes, God's judgment of s____ (*sin*) in the Bible involves d____ (*death*). This shows that God takes sin s____ (*seriously*). But he is also full of love and g____ (*grace*), and J____ (*Jesus*) proved that. God has the r____ (*right*) to give life and take it, but he's never u____ (*unfair*)."

4 Continuing the Conversation . . .

Knowing: How could you encourage a friend who is struggling to understand how God could punish sin with death? Write down one or two points that stood out to you from this conversation and practice explaining each of them out loud.

Doing: Write a letter to God expressing your honest feelings about his authority over life and death, even if you're still wrestling with it.

Sharing: Explain the two points that you wrote down and practiced in the "Knowing" activity to a friend who might think God is just angry or unfair. If you don't know anyone like this, do a role-play conversation with a family member or friend. The other person plays the role of someone who is bothered by God taking lives in the Bible, and you explain to them the points you wrote down.

5 Additional Resources

Scriptures & Print Resources:

- Scriptures: Genesis 18:22–33; 1 Samuel 2:6–10; Job 1:20–22; Psalm 103:8–14; Psalm 145:8–21; Isaiah 55:6–9; Ezekiel 33:10–20; Romans 5:6–9; Romans 6:20–23
- Book: Paul Copan, *Is God a Moral Monster?: Making Sense of the Old Testament God.* Grand Rapids, MI: Baker Books, 2011. This book answers modern accusations that the Old Testament God is cruel or unjust.
- Book: Paul Copan and Matthew Flannagan, *Did God Really Command Genocide?: Coming to Terms with the Justice of God.* Grand Rapids, MI: Baker Books, 2014. This book helps readers understand the hard-to-read Old Testament battle stories, showing that God's commands weren't about cruelty or genocide.

Online Resources:

Note: To link to these resources, click the QR code below or go to www.Renew.org/GC

- Video: William Lane Craig provides helpful context on God's commands to destroy the Canaanites.
- Video: Clay Jones provides helpful context on God's commands to destroy the Canaanites.

Why should God get so worked up over sin?

1 How would *you* answer the question, "Why should God get so worked up over sin?"

Here's the answer we'll explore:

> "It is logical to hate sin because it causes destruction. Because God hates sin and loves humanity, he paid sin's penalty, offers us forgiveness, and gives us time to accept it."

2 Now, let's walk through this answer.

Part 1: "It is logical to <u>hate</u> sin . . ."

When someone calls us out for doing something wrong—when they confront us about a sin—we usually respond in one of four ways:

Point fingers. This means blaming someone else. We might say, "Well, of course I did what I did! They made me do it!" Or it's turning the tables on the person pointing out my sin and saying, "Well, who are you to judge?" Either way, it's avoiding responsibility.

Smirk. Often, we treat sin like a joke or a humorous mistake. We laugh it off like it's no big deal. But if we were seeing clearly, we would see there's nothing funny about what our sin does to our soul, to our family, to our friendships, and especially to our relationship with God.

Shrug. This is the "whatever" response. It says, "What's the big deal? I'm a sinner, you're a sinner, everybody's a sinner. God's grace covers it; so my sin is no big deal." But this attitude forgets how serious and damaging sin actually is.

Humble ourselves and repent. This means admitting our wrongdoing and trying to change. The celebrated King David, after being discovered as an adulterer and murderer, went to God a broken man. He wrote:

> "Have mercy on me, O God,
>   according to your unfailing love;
> according to your great compassion
>   blot out my transgressions.
> Wash away all my iniquity
>   and cleanse me from my sin.
> For I know my transgressions,
>   and my sin is always before me.
> Against you, you only, have I sinned
>   and done what is evil in your sight;
> so you are right in your verdict
>   and justified when you judge." (Psalm 51:1-4)

Is one of these responses more honest and logical than the others? Yes, and this will become even more clear as we take a moment to reflect on what our sin actually *does*.

Q. What line from Psalm 51:1–4 (above) sticks out to you the most or speaks to you personally?

Part 2: "It is logical to hate sin *because it causes destruction*..."

Most of us hate suffering. But sometimes we don't stop to ask: What causes a lot of the world's suffering in the first place?

The Bible says that a huge cause of suffering is "sin." Sometimes we suffer because of our own sin (e.g., I rob a bank and go to jail). Sometimes it's because of someone else's sin (e.g., someone cheats me out of my money). But often, suffering goes all the way back to the very first sin we read about in the book of Genesis:

> "And the Lord God commanded the man, 'You are free to eat from any tree in the garden; but you must not eat from the tree of the knowledge of good and evil, for when you eat from it you will certainly die.'" (Genesis 2:16–17).

Ever since Adam and Eve, sin has messed everything up. It's affected every part of life. Now, we feel:

- Embarrassed by ourselves (Genesis 3:7)
- Afraid of God's judgment (Genesis 3:8)
- Blamed by each other (Genesis 3:12)
- Frustrated by the world around us (Genesis 3:16–19)

And even though God offers to forgive our sins, sin's *consequences* are often not erased. Here are four of those consequences.

1) When we sin, we dishonor God (2 Timothy 2:20–21). Think of it this way: A few years ago, a kind food vendor supported a protest and gave out free food to the protesters. But one day, when he couldn't bring food, some people responded by sending the vendor death threats and smearing his food carts with blood and urine. That's horrible, right? But, when we sin, we treat the free gift of God's grace like that. Instead of responding in gratitude, we smear it with filth. We take his kindness and respond with disrespect.

2) When we sin, we assist Satan (2 Timothy 2:22–26). True story: a guy saw someone struggling to carry a large TV and offered to help. But after he started to load it into the other guy's car, he got a better look at the TV and realized, "This is *my* TV!" He was helping the man steal his TV. That's what sin does. It means we're helping the enemy. We're assisting the one who seeks to steal, kill, and destroy us (John 10:10).

3) When we sin, we hurt people (2 Timothy 3:1–5). It's not just about us. Sin wrecks relationships: Affairs devastate spouses and children. Jealousy destroys friendships. Angry words wound souls. Lies wreck reputations.

4) When we sin, we oppose the truth (2 Timothy 3:8–9). When we sin, we pretend that either: 1) God doesn't see us (he's not all-present); 2) God doesn't know better than us (he's not all-knowing); or 3) God won't do anything about it (he's not all-powerful). In other words, when we sin, we act like God isn't God. We oppose the truth. And that not only makes us sinners, but fools.

So, we have every reason to hate sin. But then why do we still do it? It's because we don't just hate sin; we also love it. Proverbs 26:11 puts it this way:

> "As a dog returns to its vomit, so fools repeat their folly." (Proverbs 26:11).

We keep going back to sin because we want to. In order to stop returning to it, we have to allow higher, better desires to edge out our desires for filth.

Q. Pick a sin. What is a higher, better desire than the desire for that sin?

*Part 3: "It is logical to <u>hate</u> sin because it causes <u>destruction</u>. **Because God hates <u>sin</u> and loves <u>humanity</u> . . .**"*

When we see throughout the Bible how much God hates sin, it can honestly feel a little scary. We might fear that if he hates sin enough to send judgment on it, there might be something wrong with his character. Perhaps he doesn't love humans as much as we thought. Or perhaps he is all anger and has no kindness or gentleness.

But this isn't a logical way to look at God at all. The truth is, God hates sin *because* he loves humanity. Think of it this way: A doctor doesn't try to kill cancer in a patient's body because the doctor hates the patient. No, the doctor attacks the cancer in order to *save* the person. In the same way, God knows that sin is attacking and destroying the people he loves. Because he loves us, it makes sense that he would hate what destroys us: sin.

In 1 Peter 2:11, Peter urges Christians "to abstain from sinful desires, which wage war against your soul." That's a powerful way to think about it: our sinful desires aren't *us*; rather, they wage war *against* us. They are like a war going on inside us, trying to take us down. So it makes sense that God would seek to destroy sin in us—before sin destroys us. A big way he does this is by giving us helpful commands–rules that, if we consistently obey them, will keep us from sin and spare us from a ton of suffering. And because we have all sinned and disobeyed his rules, God took things even further. He actually stepped in to save us from sin's penalty, which we will discuss next.

Q. Read 1 Peter 2:11 again. According to this verse, what is it that sinful desires do to us? Are there any ways you have experienced this in your own life?

147

*Part 4: "It is logical to <u>hate</u> sin because it causes <u>destruction</u>. Because God hates <u>sin</u> and loves <u>humanity</u>, **he paid sin's <u>penalty</u>** . . ."*

What is sin's penalty? Romans 6:23 gives a short but powerful answer: "For the wages of sin is death." That's what sin earns: death. And what exactly is death? At its core, death is always a separation. When we use the word "death," we usually mean what happens at the end of a person's earthly life, when a person's body stops working and their soul separates from their body; what's left behind is lifeless. According to Scripture, the reason we die goes back to a punishment Adam and Eve earned when they sinned and got exiled from paradise. When they sinned, death entered the human story as part of that punishment.

Now, on the one hand, it's good that life here doesn't last forever. That's because, one day, we all will stand before God and give an account of how we lived. Knowing this should keep us humble.

But on the other hand, death isn't a good thing in itself. First Corinthians 15:26 even calls death our enemy. It says, "The last enemy to be destroyed is death." A major reason Jesus came was to destroy death's power over us by his own death on the cross. Hebrews 2:14–15 explains: "Since the children have flesh and blood, he too shared in their humanity so that by his death he might break the power of him who holds the power of death—that is, the devil—and free those who all their lives were held in slavery by their fear of death." Again, the penalty, or "wages," of sin is death, but Jesus destroys the power of death by his own death.

But there's a second kind of death the Bible talks about, and it's a much worse separation than the separation of the body from the soul. It's the eternal separation of us from God. Since God is the source of life, this is the ultimate separation. Revelation 20:14 calls this the "second death."

This is a terrifying idea, but it's also a fair one. People don't naturally want God ruling their lives, so this ultimate separation from God is actually God's way of giving people what they think they want: life without him. But here's the problem: apart from God, there can be no good thing; thus, it makes sense that this second death is called "hell."

Yet there is some amazing news in all this sadness: Jesus experienced both kinds of deaths, and he did it for us! On the cross, Jesus didn't just face physical death; he also took on the worst kind of separation, the judgment we deserve. He took our sins upon himself and faced the full wrath of God. His close and loving relationship with his Father gave way to a horrifying separation from his Father, as the Father poured out all his judgment against sin on his Son. Jesus was our substitute. His perfect relationship with the Father was broken so that ours could be restored. He paid the penalty for sin so we wouldn't have to.

When we place our faith in Jesus, an incredible transfer happens. As 2 Corinthians 5:21 says, "God made him who had no sin to be sin for us, so that in him we might become the righteousness of God." Instead of separation, Jesus offers us forever-togetherness with God.

Q. What are the two kinds of death described in the Bible? How does Jesus free us from fear when it comes to both kinds of death?

*Part 5: "It is logical to hate sin because it causes destruction. Because God hates sin and loves humanity, he paid sin's penalty, **offers us forgiveness, and gives us time to accept it.**"*

Have you ever been frustrated putting together a jigsaw puzzle? Sometimes it feels like two pieces should fit together, but no matter how hard you try, they just won't. But if you stick with it, you eventually realize every piece has a place and all the pieces do fit together. The full picture starts to make sense.

There are two "puzzle pieces" within Christianity that may feel like they just can't fit together. The first is this: God is love. He's kind, gentle, and forgiving. When he thinks about us humans, he can't help but love us because we are his special creation, his image bearers. That's the first puzzle piece: God's love.

But then there's another puzzle piece: God sometimes does scary things. In the Bible, when people willfully disobey him, he might just take their lives—even wiping out thousands of them all at once. There's the Genesis flood, the disastrous plagues on Egypt, and the fire he rained down on the cities of Sodom and Gomorrah. In the book of Joshua, God has his people destroy towns that were full of terrible sins like idolatry and child sacrifice. Later, when God's own people turned to idols and ignored him for decades, he even allowed foreign empires to invade and destroy them. And in the New Testament, we read about *eternal* judgment, where people are cast outside of God's presence forever in eternal separation from him.

So, how in the world can those two puzzle pieces fit together? How can a perfectly good, all-loving God also judge people in such scary ways?

Here's what we often forget: understanding God isn't a matter of trying to cram only two puzzle pieces together. There are more puzzle pieces to understanding God's character, and a crucial third piece that helps us see how God can be both loving and wrathful is this: God's *patience.*

God isn't *quick* to get angry. Rather, he gives people opportunity after opportunity to return to him. Numbers 14:18a says, "The Lord is slow to anger, abounding in love and forgiving sin and rebellion." This doesn't say that God never gets angry but that he's *slow* to anger. He's patient. Plus, he's eager to forgive when people repent and return to him.

When the Israelites were punished by being invaded by their enemies, they eventually realized how patient God had been all along: "For many years you were patient with them.

By your Spirit you warned them through your prophets. Yet they paid no attention, so you gave them into the hands of the neighboring peoples" (Nehemiah 9:30).

God's patience won't last forever. But the reason he waits is because he loves us and wants to forgive all our sins; he gives us time to accept his grace. Second Peter 3:9b explains his heart toward sinners: "He is patient with you, not wanting anyone to perish, but everyone to come to repentance."

So, God is full of love, which is why he patiently gives us every chance to turn to him. But because he's also just, he won't let sin and evil go on forever.

Q. Have you experienced God's patience in your own life? In what ways?

3 Can you fill in the blanks from memory?

Why should God get so worked up over sin?

"It is logical to h___ (*hate*) sin because it causes d___ (*destruction*). Because God hates s___ (*sin*) and loves h___ (*humanity*), he paid sin's p___ (*penalty*), offers us f___ (*forgiveness*), and gives us t___ (*time*) to accept it."

4 Continuing the Conversation . . .

Knowing: The prophet Jeremiah in the Old Testament looked ahead toward a new covenant that God would make with his people. In this new covenant, God says, "I will be their God, and they will be my people." He continues, "They will all know me, from the least of them to the greatest . . . for I will forgive their wickedness and will remember their sins no more" (Jeremiah 31:33b, 34:b). Knowing that God already offers you forgiveness, how should that affect your willingness to go to God when you have a sin problem?

Doing: It can be easy to miss the connection between sin and the suffering that it causes. Make a list of ten sins and then trace each sin to a type of suffering that it can cause.

Sharing: Pick someone you have influence with. If they're up for a conversation, ask them, "Does it bother you that God hates sin?" Feel free to use truth you've learned in this conversation.

5 Additional Resources

Scriptures & Print Resources:

- Scriptures: Genesis 2:16–17; Genesis 3:1–19; 2 Timothy 2:20–3:9; Proverbs 26:11; 1 Peter 2:11; 2 Corinthians 5:21; Romans 6:23; Nehemiah 9:30
- Book: Michael Strickland and Anessa Westbrook, *New Birth: Conversion and Baptism*, Renew.org, 2021. The first chapter of this short book explores why people need to be saved from their sins; the rest of the book describes what it means to place our faith in Jesus.

Online Resources:

Note: To link to these resources, click the QR code below or go to www.Renew.org/GC

- Article: Daniel McCoy, "4 Righteous Responses to Evil (and Which Ones Are in Our Job Description)." This article discusses hatred of evil, grief over evil, anger at evil, and wrath against evil and asks which are appropriate responses for disciples of Jesus.
- Article: Jeremy Bacon, "Lord's Prayer: Forgive Us Our Debts." This article explores what it means for us to pray, "Forgive us our debts as we also have forgiven our debtors."
- The Connection Pointe Worldview Website has a series that discusses what Jesus did for us on the cross and how we are made in God's image but broken by sin.

What gives God the right to judge us— especially with eternal punishment?

1 **How would *you* answer the question, "What gives God the right to judge us— especially with eternal punishment?"**

Here's the answer we'll explore:

"Hell is eternal punishment away from God's presence. Although some think hell doesn't fit with a loving God, justice demands that those who reject God's grace face punishment for their sins. God has the right to judge us and will be completely fair as the perfect judge."

2 Now, let's walk through this answer . . .

Part 1: "Hell is eternal punishment away from God's <u>presence</u> . . ."

Let's be honest, hell isn't fun to think about. It's one of the hardest topics in the Bible. Maybe you've wondered, "If God is so loving, how could he let anyone go to such a horrible place forever?" That's a fair question, and we'll explore it in this conversation. But first, we need to see that the Bible clearly teaches that hell is real, and it's a place of eternal punishment away from God's presence.

The Bible doesn't give every detail about hell, but it does tell us some important things. It's called a place of "eternal destruction" for those who reject God and ignore the sacrifice Jesus made for them (2 Thessalonians 1:8–9). Jesus describes it as "eternal fire" (Matthew 25:41), "outer darkness" (Matthew 25:30), and a place of "weeping and gnashing of teeth" (Matthew 13:42, 50).

But what makes hell truly awful is being cut off from God forever. Every good thing we enjoy—love, peace, joy, beauty, purpose—comes from him (James 1:17). Hell means total separation from God and from all good things. It means hearing God say, "Depart from me" (Matthew 7:23; Matthew 25:41) because your sins have separated you from him (Isaiah 59:2), and you've rejected his offer of rescue. That's what 2 Thessalonians 1:9 means when it says people in hell will be "away from the presence of the Lord and the glory of his might."

God doesn't give us these warnings about the reality of hell for no reason. He tells us the truth so we'll understand what happens when we choose to go our own way and take the punishment our sins deserve. Now that we've seen a bit of what the Bible says about hell, let's ask the big question: How does hell fit with a perfectly loving God?

Q. If every good thing comes from God (James 1:17), what do you think life would be like without him—forever?

*Part 2: "Hell is eternal punishment away from God's <u>presence</u>. **Although some think hell doesn't fit with a <u>loving</u> God . . ."***

If God really loves us no matter what (Romans 5:8) and his love is beyond measure (Ephesians 3:18–19), then how could he let anyone go to a place of eternal punishment? That's a question many people ask. Some say, "If I were in charge of the universe, I wouldn't be so harsh. Why not just forgive everyone and move on without the punishment?"

Others wonder if hell is just too extreme or unfair. They might ask, "Even if we do deserve some kind of punishment, why should it last forever? Our lives on earth are short. So how can a few decades of sin lead to consequences that never end? Also, why do horrible people like Hitler receive the same punishment (going to hell) as others who reject Jesus, even if those others are far less sinful than he was?"

These are honest, important questions that deserve thoughtful answers. So let's take a closer look. Why does God have to punish sin at all? And if punishment is necessary, is hell too extreme or unfair?

Q. Have you ever struggled with the idea of a loving God allowing anyone to go to hell? Why or why not?

*Part 3: "Hell is eternal punishment away from God's <u>presence</u>. Although some think hell doesn't fit with a <u>loving</u> God, **justice demands that those who reject God's grace face <u>punishment</u> for their sins . . ."***

First, let's think about why God must punish sin at all. The short answer is this: if God ignored sin and didn't punish it, then he wouldn't be just. Sometimes we forget just how serious sin really is. And we also forget that God is not only perfectly loving—he's also perfectly just and good. That means he can't overlook evil or just "let it slide." If he did, he wouldn't be good, and he wouldn't be worthy of our worship.

Deep down, we know that real justice demands that evil be punished. When terrible things happen—like abuse, racism, or murder—we instinctively know there should be consequences. So why would we expect less from a perfectly holy God? Some people complain that God doesn't stop all evil in this life. But when we hear that he *will* punish evil in the next life, others say he should just let it go. The truth is, we can't have it both ways. And honestly, we don't want a God who's soft on evil. We want a God who makes sure that justice is done.

God's love and justice actually explain why Jesus died for us. On the one hand, God's justice demands that sin be punished. But on the other hand, God's love led him to take that punishment for us. Just before Jesus was taken away to be crucified, he even asked the Father if there was another way to save us. But there wasn't (Mark 14:36). Sin had to be paid for, and Jesus chose to take our place (Colossians 2:13–14). That's how seriously God takes both sin *and* love.

God doesn't enjoy punishing anyone. In fact, 2 Peter 3:9 says he is "patient toward you, not wishing that any should perish, but that all should reach repentance." God offers grace to everyone and wants us to accept it. But if we reject that gift, we're choosing to take the punishment ourselves. His justice requires that sin be dealt with, but his love has already made a way out. It's up to you whether you let Jesus take that punishment for you or choose to take it yourself.

Q. Can you think of a time when someone wronged you or someone close to you, and you wanted justice to be done? How might that feeling help you understand why God must deal with sin and uphold justice?

Part 4: "Hell is eternal punishment away from God's <u>presence</u>. Although some think hell doesn't fit with a <u>loving</u> God, <u>justice</u> demands that those who reject God's grace face <u>punishment</u> for their sins. **God has the <u>right to</u> judge us** . . ."

Not only do we want a God who is perfectly just and punishes sin, but God is also the only one truly qualified to judge humanity. Think about it—God created us (Genesis 1:27), knows everything about us (Psalm 139:1–4), and sees not just our actions but also our thoughts and motives (Hebrews 4:12–13). Unlike human judges, who can make mistakes or be biased, God never gets it wrong. His judgment is always right because he is perfectly holy, wise, and just (Deuteronomy 32:4).

We also learned in *Conversation 3* how it makes sense that God himself is the standard for right and wrong. He didn't just make up some random list of rules. Right and wrong flow from who he is—his perfectly good and holy character. That means he's not only the Creator but also the moral lawgiver. So when we sin, we're rebelling against the One who made us and gives us every breath (Acts 17:25), and the One who defines what is truly good (Mark 10:18; 1 John 1:5). Because of who he is, he has every right to hold us accountable.

That might sound intimidating, but it's actually good news. If God didn't have the right to judge, we'd be stuck in a world where evil often wins and justice is never guaranteed. But because God is perfectly just. We can trust that his judgment will always be fair. When God judges us, no one will be wrongly condemned, and no sin will be ignored. In the end, perfect justice will be done—just as it should be.

Q. How would it be different to stand before God as your judge rather than standing before a human judge? Since God will one day hold you accountable, how does that change the way you live? How should it draw us to Jesus?

*Part 5: "Hell is eternal punishment away from God's <u>presence</u>. Although some think hell doesn't fit with a <u>loving</u> God, <u>justice</u> demands that those who reject God's grace face <u>punishment</u> for their sins. God has the <u>right</u> to judge us **and will be completely <u>fair</u> as the perfect <u>judge</u>.***"

We've seen that it's a good thing that God holds us accountable for our sin, and we've discussed how God has the right to judge us. Now let's look at the concerns we mentioned earlier about hell being too extreme.

One concern is that hell shouldn't be eternal, since we only commit a limited number of sins in our short time on earth. But we need to remember that sin isn't just about *how many* wrong things we do. It's also about *the seriousness* of the sin and *the One we're sinning against.* Even in human courts, the punishment for a crime isn't based only on how long it took to commit the crime or how many crimes were committed; what matters most is how serious the crime was. Some crimes are so severe that they lead to life sentences or even the death penalty. In a similar way, rejecting the God who created and loves us is extremely serious. And even when it comes to the number of sins, don't forget this: people in hell probably don't stop sinning. So, we shouldn't assume that people in hell are only punished for the sins they did on earth. Their sins continue, and so does the punishment.

Another concern is that there shouldn't be one punishment. How is it fair that everyone who rejects Jesus as their Savior goes to the same place regardless of how sinful their lives were? The good news is that the Bible teaches there are different levels of punishment in hell. Even though everyone who rejects Jesus faces separation from God, not everyone is punished the same. Jesus said judgment will be "according to what they have done" (2 Corinthians 5:10). He also said some will receive "many blows" and others "few" depending on what they knew and how they responded (Luke 12:47–48). Some will be punished "more severely" (Mark 12:40; Hebrews 10:29), and Jesus said it will be "more bearable" for some on judgment day (Matthew 11:21–24). So, God's justice takes everything into account—our knowledge, choices, and circumstances.

In the end, God will be completely fair. In fact, he'll be more than fair. No one will be punished more than they deserve, and those who accept Jesus and let him take their penalty will receive far better than they deserve. That's justice and grace working together, and it's exactly what we'd expect from a God who is both perfectly just and perfectly loving.

Q. God judges each person fairly and takes into account their own situation. How does that affect the way you think about his justice?

3 Can you fill in the blanks from memory?

What gives God the right to judge us—especially with eternal punishment?

"Hell is eternal punishment away from God's p___ (*presence*). Although some think hell doesn't fit with a l___ (*loving*) God, j___ (*justice*) demands that those who reject God's grace face p___ (*punishment*) for their sins. God has the r___ (*right*) to judge us and will be completely f___ (*fair*) as the perfect j___ (*judge*)."

4 Continuing the Conversation . . .

Knowing: Imagine a friend says, "I can't believe in a God who would send people to hell. A loving God wouldn't give us such an extreme punishment." Based on what you've learned, write down 2–3 key points you would share with your friend. Practice saying them out loud.

Doing: Discuss with God (out loud or in a letter) your feelings about his justice and love. Thank Jesus for taking the penalty for your sins so that you can be saved.

Sharing: Start a conversation with a non-Christian friend by asking, "Have you ever wondered how a loving God could allow hell?" Or practice by doing a role-play with a friend or family member who takes the view that God shouldn't send anyone to hell.

Share what you learned in this conversation (especially the points you wrote down in the "Knowing" activity).

5 Additional Resources

Scriptures & Print Resources:

- Scriptures: Deuteronomy 32:4; Psalm 139:1–4; Isaiah 6:3; Isaiah 59:1–2; Habakkuk 1:13; Matthew 7:21–23; Matthew 11:21–24; Matthew 13:36–43, 47–50; Matthew 25:30–46; Mark 12:40; Luke 12:47–48; Romans 1:18; Romans 2:5–6; Romans 3:23; Romans 5:8; Romans 6:23; 2 Corinthians 5:10; Ephesians 3:18–19; Colossians 2:13–14; 2 Thessalonians 1:5–10; 2 Peter 3:8–9; Hebrews 4:12–13; Hebrews 10:29–31; James 4:12
- Book: Paul Copan, *That's Just Your Interpretation: Responding to Skeptics Who Challenge Your Faith.* Grand Rapids, MI: Baker Books, 2001. See chapter 11, which addresses a number of objections related to God and hell.

Online Resources:

Note: To link to these resources, click the QR code below or go to www.Renew.org/GC

- The Connection Pointe Worldview Website has a series that discusses what the Bible says about heaven and hell.
- Video: William Lane Craig addresses the question of how a loving God could send anyone to hell.
- Article: A "Room For Doubt" article offers additional details on a loving God allowing hell.

If we love God as Father, doesn't that go against fearing God as King?

1 How would *you* answer the question, "If we love God as Father, doesn't that go against fearing God as King?"

Here's the answer we'll explore:

> "Anyone in the Bible who saw God's power became afraid, and this fear is the beginning of wisdom. Loving God starts with recognizing who he is and receiving his amazing grace."

2 Now, let's walk through this answer.

Part 1: "Anyone in the Bible who saw God's power became afraid . . ."

The prophet Isaiah was given a vision of God in heaven. God was on a throne, high and exalted, and surrounding him were angels calling to each other "Holy, holy, holy is the LORD Almighty; the whole earth is full of his glory!" (Isaiah 6:3). And guess what Isaiah felt in that moment? It wasn't a warm and fuzzy feeling, like joy or peace. Instead, it was pure awe and fear. The scene was overwhelming, with smoke filling the room and the angels' booming voices shaking the room's foundations. Isaiah was filled with dread, as he cried out, "Woe to me! I am ruined! For I am a man of unclean lips, and I live among a people of unclean lips, and my eyes have seen the King, the LORD Almighty" (Isaiah 6:5).

That was in the Old Testament. But in the New Testament, something similar happened to one of Jesus' closest friends, the apostle John. After Jesus had risen from the dead and returned to heaven, John got a vision of Jesus. It was a revelation about Jesus and what was to come—which is why we call what John wrote down the "book of Revelation." Instead of Jesus the carpenter or Jesus the teacher, this was a vision of Jesus in all his majestic, heavenly glory. This moment was so powerful and intense that even though John had spent years with Jesus and knew Jesus well, he writes, "When I saw him, I fell at his feet as though dead" (Revelation 1:17).

Every time someone in the Bible saw God's power and glory, their first response was fear.

But that's not how their stories end. For example, when John fell on his face before Jesus, immediately Jesus came to him, put his hand on him, and said, "Do not be afraid." He reminded John that he (Jesus) is the First and the Last, the One who is alive forever. Fearing God is certainly not meant to be our *only* reaction to God, especially since we are called to receive his grace and be part of his family. But a healthy relationship with God does start with recognizing who he is: the King, the Lord Almighty.

Q. Read Exodus 33:18–20. What was God's warning to Moses?

Part 2: "Anyone in the <u>Bible</u> who saw God's <u>power</u> became <u>afraid</u>, **and this** **fear is the beginning of <u>wisdom</u>***. . ."*

Russian author Alexander Solzhenitsyn was thrown in prison by the Communist Soviet Union for speaking out against its leader, Joseph Stalin, and against communism. The founder of communism, Karl Marx, hated religion and built communism around atheism. Years later, after Solzhenitsyn got out of prison, he was kicked out of Russia and gave a famous speech at Buckingham Palace in London. He said that he'd spent fifty years researching the destruction of his nation and trying to figure out how it all happened. How did his country fall apart, resulting in the suffering and death of millions of people? After all that research, he summed it up in just one sentence:

> "If I were asked today to formulate as concisely as possible the main cause of the ruinous revolution that swallowed up some 60 million of our people, I could not put it more accurately than to repeat: 'Men have forgotten God; that's why all this has happened.'"[18]

What happens when we forget about God? What happens when we live as though he doesn't exist, and we just do whatever feels right? Usually, when powerful people forget who God is, they start pretending like *they* are god. Instead of respecting the rules God gave us to live by, they start making their own rules about what's right and wrong. Instead of recognizing the world as God's creation, the world becomes their playground. Powerful people start mistreating the weak and remaking the world according to their own desires. But when people think they don't need God, they forget something huge: humans make really bad gods. When given a lot of power, we tend to misuse it and hurt ourselves and others. When you subtract wisdom from your life, you get stupidity. When you subtract God from your wisdom, you get tyranny.

This is why the Bible says fearing God is the beginning of wisdom. If we don't respect God with reverential fear, it's like a young kid who ignores his dad's rules about power tools or ladders or even guns. The kid says, "I don't need Dad telling me what to do! I can do it myself!" What's going to happen if that kid ignores his dad's rules for long enough? He's going to hurt himself and others. It's the same when we ignore God and don't take him seriously.

Q. Read Proverbs 1:7. According to this proverb, what's the opposite of fearing God and becoming wise?

*Part 3: "Anyone in the <u>Bible</u> who saw God's <u>power</u> became <u>afraid</u>, and this <u>fear</u> is the beginning of <u>wisdom</u>. **Loving God** . . ."*

How important is it that we love God? When someone asked Jesus what the most important commandment was in the entire Old Testament law, notice how Jesus answered:

> "One of the teachers of the law came and heard them debating. Noticing that Jesus had given them a good answer, he asked him, 'Of all the commandments, which is the most important?' 'The most important one,' answered Jesus, 'is this: 'Hear, O Israel: The Lord our God, the Lord is one. Love the Lord your God with all your heart and with all your soul and with all your mind and with all your strength.'" (Mark 12:28–30)

So, it's pretty obvious from Jesus that loving God isn't just important—it's the most important thing we can be doing with our lives. Now, based on Jesus' words, *how* should we love God? Jesus used four words to describe what parts of us ought to be involved in loving God. The *heart* is the center of our emotional, spiritual, and mental life. The *soul* is the center of who we are—our inner self. The mind is the part of us that thinks, understands, and reasons. Our *strength* is our energy, effort, and abilities. You may have noticed that these four parts of us overlap, almost like shingles on a roof overlap each other to prevent rainwater from coming through. And that's the point: Jesus said to love God with *all* of who we are—*all* our heart, soul, mind, and strength. No part of us is left out.

So loving God isn't just about offering a sacrifice or praying a prayer or singing a song or even just "liking" God because he's nice to us. It's much bigger than that. It means every part of our being is focused on loving him.

Some of us need to be reminded that loving God is not just feeling love toward God; it also means obeying his commandments. Others of us need to be reminded that loving God is not just obeying his commandments; it also means feeling love and adoration toward God.

Imagine this: A husband comes home from work on the couple's anniversary and hands his wife a dozen red roses. She smiles and says, "Oh honey! That is so sweet!" And the husband replies, "Don't mention it. That's what I'm supposed to do, after all. And look, I think I have a note too. Let me read it." He pulls out a note from his pocket. "Yes, I wrote this note, and it says, 'Happy anniversary.' There. I did it." Now, the roses and kind words are important. But without the real feelings, they just sort of wilt, don't they?

In the same way, if we talk to God, sing to God, or obey Almighty God without any feelings of reverence or wonder or gratitude, then it's like handing him flowers from a wilted soul. Likewise, just *feeling* love toward God doesn't mean much if we don't take his commands seriously. As Jesus told his disciples, "If you love me, keep my commands" (John 14:15).

Q. Can you recite the four "alls" that Jesus says we are meant to love God with?

Part 4: "Anyone in the <u>Bible</u> who saw God's <u>power</u> became <u>afraid</u>, and this <u>fear</u> is the beginning of <u>wisdom</u>. Loving <u>God</u> **starts with <u>recognizing</u> who he is . . ."**

How could we possibly be expected to love God all the time with all our being—as in, all of our heart, soul, mind, and strength? That feels impossible sometimes. But thankfully, God doesn't love us because we're so great at loving him. We're loved by God *despite* our inability to consistently live the right ways. But we are created to love God in these ways, and it must be something we aim for; otherwise, Jesus wouldn't make it an expectation of his followers.

The good news is that, as followers of Jesus, we learn how to live by watching his life and listening to his teachings. Jesus showed us what it looks like to live completely devoted to God. So, if you aren't doing a great job of loving God (and honestly, none of us do it perfectly), the best place to start is by looking at Jesus and learning from him.

And here's something even more amazing: not only did Jesus live a life devoted to his Father, but he also did a perfect job of showing us what the Father is like. That means the more we get to know Jesus, the better we understand who God is—and the more reasons we'll find to love him. It becomes much easier to love God once you start to see his wisdom, love, majesty, creativity, justice, power, and so on.

Q. When is the last time you took a minute to reflect on who God is? Take a minute and do that now, perhaps making a list of what God is like, based on what we've seen in Jesus.

*Part 5: "Anyone in the <u>Bible</u> who saw God's <u>power</u> became <u>afraid</u>, and this <u>fear</u> is the beginning of <u>wisdom.</u> Loving <u>God</u> starts with <u>recognizing</u> who he is **and <u>receiving his amazing grace.</u>"**

A strange thing happens when somebody does fear God. This strange thing happened to Isaiah when he saw God and thought he would die. It also happened to John when he saw Jesus and thought he would die. It even shows up in Luke 12, where Jesus says to fear God because he has the power to send you to hell. And it's this: Right after the person listening gets really scared, they are told to stop being afraid. Each is basically told, "Okay, now don't be afraid. You're going to be fine."

The fear of the Lord, that reverential respect and awe for God, is just the beginning. It's the foundation. It's got to be there. It makes good sense, and it needs to stay in place.

But let's say that fear is there. Let's say you really do respect God, as you realize he has all-power, is totally righteous, created everything, and is beyond brilliant. With that kind of foundation in place, imagine hearing that this all-powerful God loves you, forgives you of your sins, and welcomes you into his family as his beloved child. Suddenly, that news isn't something to yawn about; it becomes the best news you've ever heard.

Q. How would you explain the connection between fearing God and loving him?

3 Can you fill in the blanks from memory?

If we love God as Father, doesn't that go against fearing God as King?

"Anyone in the B____ (*Bible*) who saw God's p____ (*power*) became a____ (*afraid*), and this f____ (*fear*) is the beginning of w____ (*wisdom*). Loving G____ (*God*) starts with r____ (*recognizing*) who he is and r____ (*receiving*) his amazing g____ (*grace*)."

4 Continuing the Conversation . . .

Knowing: Take a moment to revisit what it means to love God with all your heart, soul, mind, and strength. (We discussed this in Part 3 of this conversation.) What are some real-life ways you can live that out? Try to come up with more than one specific example from your own life.

Doing: Following the pattern of Isaiah and John, take some time to pray to God. As they did, start with acknowledging his power and might. Then thank him for his love and mercy. Finally, take time to tell him you love him.

Sharing: Pick someone in your circle of influence and ask them if they think it's possible to fear God and love him at the same time. Using truth from this conversation, offer your own thoughts on how the two fit together according to the Bible.

5 Additional Resources

Scriptures & Print Resources:

- Scriptures: Isaiah 6; Revelation 1:9–20; Exodus 33:18–20; Proverbs 1:1–7; Mark 12:28–30; Luke 12:4–7
- Book: A. W. Tozer, *The Pursuit of God.* Chicago: Moody Publishers, 2006. This classic book is a thoughtful primer on why God is fully worth our time and trust.

Online Resources:

Note: To link to these resources, click the QR code below or go to www.Renew.org/GC

- Article: Jeremy Bacon, "Sermon on the Mount: What Is Love in Christianity?" This article asks what exactly is entailed in Jesus' command to love our enemies.

- Article: Daniel McCoy, "If God Is Love, Hell Is Real." This article looks at sobering implications of God's love, such as giving humans freedom and bringing about justice.

Will God save a serial killer who believes in Jesus?

1 How would *you* answer the question, "Will God save a serial killer who believes in Jesus?"

Here's the answer we'll explore:

> "In the Bible, God saves unlikely people, even those guilty of terrible sins. We are saved by God's grace, not by being less of a sinner than others. But habitual sin is dangerous, and not everyone awakens to their need for a Savior."

2 Now, let's walk through this answer.

Part 1: "In the Bible, God saves <u>unlikely</u> people . . ."

Jesus would have made a lousy politician. Politicians have to get elected, and to get elected, they need to impress important people in order to get their support. Less-than-principled politicians might say and do whatever is needed to win over different groups and get into power. And if they accidentally say something that offends a group they're trying to win over, it might destroy their chances.

But this isn't how Jesus acted at all. For example, as Jesus' ministry was starting up, he went back to his hometown of Nazareth. He was invited to preach in their synagogue, and at first, everything was going well; people were impressed, and everyone spoke well of him. After all, Jesus was the hometown boy, and they were proud to be able to claim him. But instead of only talking about how important *they*—his fellow Jews—were to God, he began to explain that God also wanted to do great things for their enemies. He mentioned two places the hometown crowd absolutely hated—Sidon and Syria—as a couple places where God had done miraculous things in the past. That did it. The hometown crowd went from excited to furious. They even tried to throw him off a cliff! But Jesus wasn't trying to be popular; he wanted to make it clear that God cares about unlikely people.

Jesus did stuff like this all the time. One time, in a crowd of people who would have been his adoring fans, Jesus singled out a guy they all hated, a chief tax collector named Zacchaeus. Instead of attacking Zaccheus, Jesus announced that this was the guy he wanted to hang out with. Another time, he was invited to the house of a respected religious leader (a Pharisee). Jesus could have seen it as an opportunity to woo this respectable person over to the Jesus movement. Instead, when a sinful woman interrupted the dinner in order to anoint Jesus' feet, it didn't matter that the Pharisee was offended by her presence. Jesus took it as an opportunity to teach the Pharisee that the sinful woman was closer to God's kingdom than the Pharisee was.

So, instead of being a politician who might say what it takes to get votes, Jesus was a Savior looking for sinners who knew they needed saving. Time after time, Jesus showed that God's love is powerful enough to save the unlikeliest of people.

Q. Read Mark 2:17. What kind of people did Jesus come to save? Would you categorize yourself as sick or healthy when it comes to needing Jesus?

Part 2: "In the Bible, God saves <u>unlikely</u> people, **even those guilty of <u>terrible</u> sins . . ."**

There's a story told of two brothers who were notorious scoundrels. They were both mean, dishonest, and no one trusted them. When one brother died, the other bribed the preacher: He would pay the preacher a lot of money if the preacher would call his brother a "saint" during the funeral. The preacher thought hard about it. He didn't want to lie, but he really could use the money. When the funeral came, he stood and started the eulogy this way: "This man was not a good man. If you knew him, you knew that he was mean, he cheated people, he drank too much, and he did all sorts of unspeakable things." He paused and added, "But compared to *his brother,* this man was a saint."

Now, that makes us wonder: Does it really make sense to compare sins and say *this* sin is worse than *that* sin, or *this* sinner is worse than *that* sinner? Can a Christian say that some sins are terrible, while others aren't as bad? Aren't all sins equally bad?

Actually, throughout the Bible, we see that not all sins are equally bad or dangerous—some are worse than others. Proverbs 6:6–19 singles out seven sins that God especially hates. In the New Testament, there are a few times when Jesus compares two groups and says one is guiltier than the other, even though both were guilty of sin (see John 19:11; Luke 10:13). And while Jesus hung around sinful people all the time, the ones who made him the angriest were religious insiders who made it harder for religious outsiders to connect with God (see Matthew 21:12). Plus, Jesus directly said that some of God's laws held more weight than others (Matthew 23:23).

But here's the good news: Even though some sins are worse than others, Jesus is totally willing to forgive them all. We could all agree that crucifying the Son of God and then laughing about it is probably the worst thing a person could ever do, and yet Jesus looked out over the crowd responsible for crucifying him and prayed, "Father, forgive them, for they do not know what they are doing" (Luke 23:34).

And don't forget the two thieves who were crucified alongside Jesus. At first, they were both making fun of Jesus, along with the rest of the crowd (Matthew 27:44). But then, one thief had a change of heart and asked Jesus, "Remember me when you come into your kingdom." Jesus responded, "Truly I tell you, today you will be with me in paradise" (Luke 23:42–43).

So we know from the Bible that Jesus is able and eager to save unlikely people, including people guilty of terrible sins.

Q. Read 1 Timothy 1:15–16. According to Paul, why did God show him so much mercy?

*Part 3: "In the Bible, God saves <u>unlikely</u> people, even those guilty of <u>terrible</u> sins. **We are saved by God's grace, not by being less of a <u>sinner</u> than others** . . ."*

Let's say you're traveling back home from an out-of-town baseball game. It's dark, and your family is driving along the highway when your dad suddenly says, "Oh great." You glance up and notice a red light on the dashboard that wasn't there before. The car slows down and pulls over to the side of the highway. As the car comes to a stop, your dad pops the hood and asks you to reach behind you and find the flashlight. Beside the toolbox, you find the flashlight and hand it to your dad. Flashlight in hand, he gets out of the car, raises the hood, and shines it on the engine. It's clear that there's a problem with the engine. But is your dad going to use the flashlight to actually fix the engine problem? No, he is going to use the flashlight to *discover* the problem. The flashlight shows what the problem is, but the flashlight is not the tool he will use to actually fix it.[19]

Now think back to the Ten Commandments—the rules God gave the ancient Israelites, like *do not murder, do not lie, do not steal,* etc. The Ten Commandments are a summary of the Old Testament rules the Bible calls the "Law." They are God's rules, so they're incredibly valuable; but they are like a flashlight. You and I are kind of like a car that has broken down, except that we are broken down because of sin.

As we've seen, a flashlight doesn't fix the problem, but it shows what the problem is. Like a powerful flashlight, the Law shines into our hearts and reveals the ways we fall short. It doesn't save us, but it shows us all the ways that we are sinners and that we need God's help. When we look at our lives through the Law, we say, "Wow, I'm a sinner!" It shows us that we need Someone to fix our problem: Jesus. Jesus is the One who actually saves us, forgiving us and guiding us in how to live.

Now is it possible that when you look at your life through the "flashlight" of God's Law, you see that you're actually doing okay in some areas? Sure. Maybe you're doing better than some of your friends when it comes to saying no to this or that sin. Or, at the very least, you're doing way better than some of those moral monsters you read about in the news, like serial killers. But if you think that keeping *some* of the Law is what saves you from your sins, you're using the "flashlight" the wrong way. Remember, the flashlight doesn't fix your problem; it shows you your problem. And if you're honest with yourself and keep looking long enough, the "flashlight" will show that you've got plenty of your own sin issues you struggle with.

Thank God that we're not saved by being less of a sinner than others—because, as Romans 3:23 says, "we *all* have sinned and fall short of the glory of God." And Romans 3:10 reminds us, "There is no one righteous, not even one." That's why we need grace—not just help, but a Savior. Praise God that we are saved by what Jesus did—and not because we're a few inches ahead of the next person.

Q. If someone asked you why God gave his people all those rules in the Old Testament, how would you answer?

Part 4: "In the Bible, God saves <u>unlikely</u> people, even those guilty of <u>terrible</u> sins. We are saved by God's <u>grace</u>, not by being less of a <u>sinner</u> than others. **But <u>habitual</u> sin is <u>dangerous</u>** . . ."

So far, we've said that God saves unlikely people, even those who are guilty of terrible sins. So does that mean it really doesn't matter what we do, because in the end God will forgive us anyway? As Romans 6:1 asks, "Shall we go on sinning so that grace may increase?" Paul answers his own question by saying, "By no means! We are those who have died to sin; how can we live in it any longer?"

So what should be our reaction to sin? We *die* to it. That's how seriously disciples of Jesus are to take their sin. When we're baptized, we're acting out the death and resurrection of Jesus by dying to our old, sinful self and rising to a new life. But why such a dramatic response? Why die to our old self? It's because sin is highly dangerous. And habitual, ongoing sin is even more dangerous.

Let's say I think to myself, *"It doesn't really matter what I do—because in the end God forgives me."* Is that an intelligent belief to have? No, that kind of belief is like poison to our soul. The truth is, ongoing, deliberate sin is spiritually toxic for our hearts. The Bible says that ongoing, deliberate sin actually "hardens" our hearts. Sin makes us "hardhearted."

Hard hearts are frightening. Imagine that I'm your doctor, and you come in and say, "I've been checking medical sites on the internet, and I think based on my symptoms, I've got a 'hard heart.' That's not a big deal, is it? It doesn't lead to other problems, right?" If I were your doctor, I would have to sit you down and explain that I don't have good news for you. I'd explain that, if left untreated, a hard heart leads to some really devastating conditions for the rest of the body.

Here are a few more metaphors used throughout the Bible for what hardheartedness does. Hardheartedness can lead to "eyes" that don't see and "ears" that don't hear (Ezekiel 12:1–2). It can lead to "depraved minds" (Romans 1:28). It leads to "stiff necks," so we eventually don't look up anymore when God tries to get our attention (Nehemiah 9:17, 29; Jeremiah 17:23). Proverbs 29:1 puts it bluntly: "Whoever remains stiff-necked after many rebukes will suddenly be destroyed—without remedy."

It's true that God graciously promises to forgive our sins when we repent and turn to him. But ongoing, deliberate sin still has the effect of hardening our hearts to God, and that's a very dangerous place to be. So, let's not be relaxed about sin, thinking, "Hey, it doesn't matter what I do, because God will forgive me." The only intelligent response to sin for disciples of Jesus is to die to it.

Q. If you start to notice that you have been having a hard heart toward God, what should you do?

*Part 5: "In the Bible, God saves <u>unlikely</u> people, even those guilty of <u>terrible</u> sins. We are saved by God's <u>grace</u>, not by being less of a <u>sinner</u> than others. But <u>habitual</u> sin is <u>dangerous</u>, **and not everyone <u>awakens to their need for a Savior</u>.**"*

You know how God saves us by grace and not by how "good" we are? For most of us, that sounds like good news. But a lot of people aren't fans of that arrangement at all. They actually wish God saved people based on a merit system—like grades in school. They think God should save the people who've worked hard to avoid the really bad sins. They dislike the idea that a really bad person, like a serial killer, could be in heaven because they accepted God's grace and placed faith in Jesus, whereas someone who seems like a relatively decent and moral person might not be in heaven because they never turned to Jesus. They wonder, "How is that fair?"

But the truth is, not everybody awakens to their need for a Savior. Sometimes, the obviously bad person realizes, "You know what? I'm a sinner! I need God so badly!" But other people—those who seem to be living a much better life—can get prideful and think, "I don't need a Savior! I'm doing just fine with my life." Jesus explained that he came for the people who know they are sinners. He used the example of a doctor and said, "It is not the healthy who need a doctor, but the sick. I have not come to call the righteous, but sinners" (Mark 2:17).

Jesus even told a parable to the religious leaders in Israel to make this point. In the story, a father tells two sons to go work in the vineyard. The first son says, "No," but then later changes his mind and works in the vineyard. The second son says, "Sure, Dad," but then later changes his mind and doesn't end up working. Jesus asks, "Which of the two did what his father wanted?" They answered, "The first." Then Jesus hit those religious leaders with a very hard truth and explained the point of the parable. He told them that the "tax collectors and prostitutes"—the people everyone else looked down on—were "entering the kingdom of God ahead of [them]" (Matthew 21:31b). Why? It's because the religious leaders *acted* like they were following God, but they weren't actually doing what God wanted: they weren't willing to repent and believe in Jesus. The so-called "bad" people admitted they were wrong and turned to God, while the "good" people were too proud to see their need for grace.

Q. Are you currently awake to your need for a Savior? Why or why not?

3 Can you fill in the blanks from memory?

Will God save a serial killer who believes in Jesus?

"In the Bible, God saves u____ (*unlikely*) people, even those guilty of t____ (*terrible*) sins. We are saved by God's g____ (*grace*), not by being less of a s____ (*sinner*) than others. But h____ (*habitual*) sin is d____ (*dangerous*), and not everyone a____ (*awakens*) to their need for a S____ (*Savior*)."

4 Continuing the Conversation . . .

Knowing: Take a few minutes to reflect on this: One of the most important warnings discussed in this conversation is that not everyone awakens to their need for a Savior. This could describe the person involved in dangerous, habitual sin since that has a hardening effect on a person's heart. But it could also describe the "good" person who is offended by the idea that they are in a dangerous spiritual position without Jesus. Here's your challenge: Ask yourself honestly: Am I fully awake to my need for Jesus? Have I ever been numb to my sin (or proud of my goodness) and missed how much I need a Savior? Write down your thoughts or share with someone you trust.

Doing: Take a minute or two and pray for God to reveal to you any areas in which you have a hard heart toward God. Perhaps you are angry at him for something he did or didn't do. Or perhaps you are resentful that he wants to be king over an area of your life that you want him to leave alone. Or perhaps you are apathetic toward him, preferring to live life without having to think about him. Pray for God to open your eyes to any hardheartedness, and then ask him to soften your heart in each of those areas.

Sharing: Is there somebody you know who is weighed down by guilt for something from their past? Ask them how they are doing and share with them what you learned about how God shows grace even to unlikely people. Even if they already know about God's grace, it's helpful to remind them that it's by God's grace that we are saved, not by being better than the next person.

5 Additional Resources

Scriptures & Print Resources:

- Scriptures: Mark 2:17; John 19:11; Luke 10:13; Matthew 21:2; Matthew 23:23; Luke 23:34; Luke 23:42–43; 1 Timothy 1:15–16; Romans 3:10; Romans 3:23; Ezekiel 12:1–2; Nehemiah 9:17, 29; Jeremiah 17:23; Proverbs 29:1

- Book: Philip Yancey, *What's So Amazing About Grace?* Grand Rapids: Zondervan Books, 2023. This book explores the beauty and scandal of the forgiveness and favor God offers to sinners.

Online Resources:

Note: To link to these resources, click the QR code below or go to www.Renew.org/GC

- Article: Bobby Harrington, "How Can I Be Forgiven When I Sin Again and Again?" This article asks what it means to live in the "light" even when we struggle with ongoing temptation.
- Article: Daniel McCoy, "A Simple Definition of Grace? Yeah, About That…" This article walks through multiple facets of God's grace we learn from the Bible.
- Article: Daniel McCoy, "What's the Worst Sin? A Good Question That's Killing Us." This article asks whether some sins are worse than others and which sins might be at the top of the list.
- Article: G. W. Steel, "Encountering God's Amazing Grace." This article explores God's grace and its implications for how we live as disciples of Jesus.

PRIVACY.FLOWCODE.COM

The Problem of Evil and Suffering

Can we believe in a powerful and loving God when the world has so much suffering and evil?

1 How would *you* answer the question, "Can we believe in a powerful and loving God when the world has so much suffering and evil?"

Here's the answer we'll explore:

> "Suffering and evil make it hard for some to believe in God. It was once commonly claimed that suffering and evil disprove God, but almost no philosophers believe this anymore. Today, some still argue that suffering and evil at least make it unlikely that God exists, but there are good reasons to keep believing in God despite all the evil and suffering."

2 Now, let's walk through this answer . . .

*Part 1: "**Suffering and evil make it hard for some to believe in God** . . ."*

Every day, our world is filled with sadness, suffering, and evil—starving children, people murdered and killed in war, innocent lives lost to natural disasters, and families torn apart by cancer and other diseases. It's obvious that our world is broken. And suffering and evil are not just academic ideas that affect some people "out there"; they affect us all deeply. If there's anything we can know for sure about our world, it's that it isn't the way it should be.

This can make it hard to understand how God fits into the picture. If there's a God who is good and powerful, why would he allow so much suffering and evil?

This is one of the toughest questions people wrestle with. In fact, the biggest reason many atheists give for not believing in God is that they don't think it makes sense to believe in a good and loving God who allows the suffering and evil we see in our world. So let's explore this difficult question, beginning with the claim that suffering and evil actually disprove the existence of God.

Q. What are some examples of suffering or evil you see in the world today? Do they make it hard for you to believe in God or trust God? Why or why not?

*Part 2: "Suffering and evil make it hard for some to believe in God. **It was once commonly claimed that suffering and evil disprove God** . . ."*

The boldest argument against the existence of God is the idea that suffering and evil prove that God doesn't exist. It's the "boldest" because it argues that suffering and evil make God's existence not just unlikely, but impossible. We'll call this the "no way" claim because it says that God doesn't fit with suffering and evil—if suffering and evil exist, then there's "no way" God can exist.[20] The reasoning behind this is simple:

- If God exists, he must be *all-powerful*. So he is *able* to stop suffering and evil.
- If God is also *perfectly* loving, he would want to stop suffering and evil.
- So, if God is both all-powerful and perfectly loving, he *must be able and willing* to stop suffering and evil. There should be *no suffering or evil if God exists*.
- But suffering and evil clearly exist in the world.
- So, God does not exist.

If this reasoning were correct, it would be very concerning to those of us who believe in God. We all know that suffering and evil are real, and if God would never allow any suffering or evil, then that's a strong reason to doubt whether there is a God.

For a long time, this reasoning seemed correct to many people. In fact, many philosophers and thinkers believed it. (Philosophers study and discuss the big questions about life, like questions about God and evil.) But that all began to change in the last fifty years or so, and a big reason for that is a Christian philosopher named Alvin Plantinga. Plantinga showed that there is a big problem with the "no way" claim. As a result, most philosophers today no longer accept it. Next, we'll see why this claim is now widely rejected.

Q. In your own words, how would you explain the reasoning behind the "no way" claim? Before moving on to the next section, what are some reasons you think this claim might be wrong?

*Part 3: "Suffering and <u>evil</u> make it hard for some to believe in <u>God</u>. It was once commonly claimed that suffering and evil <u>disprove</u> God, **but almost <u>no</u> philosophers believe this anymore** . . ."*

To see a huge problem with the "no way" claim, let's first think for a moment about free will (the ability to make our own choices). Can you think of reasons why God might want us to have free will? For one, without free will, we'd be like robots—unable to love God or each other. If you programmed a robot to say every day that it loves you, that wouldn't really be love. Love is a choice. So, one reason God might give us free will is so that we can truly love or reject him—we can choose to do good or evil.

In 1974, Alvin Plantinga shot down the "no way" claim by focusing on free will.[21] He explained that a perfectly good and powerful God might allow evil because he gave us the freedom to make our own choices. If we have free will, suffering and evil may be unavoidable.

Here's Plantinga's key point: a loving God may have good reasons for giving us free will; and if God does allow us to make our own decisions, then he can't step in and force us to always choose what's right. For all we know, it's possible that every single person with free will would choose to do evil at some point. So, since God can't *force* us to *freely* do what is good (it's impossible for free will to be forced), evil (and the suffering that goes along with it) may be an unavoidable consequence of giving us free will.

We could say more about why the "no way" claim fails, but this is enough. Even though God is all-powerful and could certainly eliminate all evil and suffering, that may require taking away our freedom. And a perfectly good and loving God may have good reasons not to do that (such as allowing us to be able to love). So, God could possibly exist even though there is evil and suffering.

Q. Does it make sense to you that a perfectly good and powerful God would give humanity the ability to make free choices, even though this allows us to do evil and cause suffering?

*Part 4: "Suffering and evil make it hard for some to believe in God. It was
once commonly claimed that suffering and evil disprove God, but almost no
philosophers believe this anymore. **Today, some still argue that suffering
and evil at least make it unlikely that God exists . . ."***

Okay, so we've seen that God may have a good reason to allow *some* suffering and evil. But why does there have to be so *much* of it? And why does it have to be so *bad*—so painful? Sometimes it even seems like a lot of suffering is pointless—nothing good comes from it at all.

This brings us to a different kind of question, which we'll call the "slim chance" claim: even if suffering and evil don't disprove God, isn't it *very unlikely* that God exists when we consider how much horrible evil there is in the world and how pointless some of it seems?[22] After all, if a good, all-powerful God existed, wouldn't we expect less pain and more good in the world? Wouldn't there be a lot less cancer and far fewer murders? Wouldn't we never see random acts of violence that don't seem to serve any higher purpose?

So, let's explore this further. While the "slim chance" claim raises a tough challenge, we'll see that it shouldn't make us doubt God's existence.

Q. Think about a time when you or someone you know experienced suffering that felt unfair or pointless (nothing good seemed to come from it). Do you have a hard time understanding why God would allow this? Explain.

*Part 5: "Suffering and evil make it hard for some to believe in God. It was
once commonly claimed that suffering and evil disprove God, but almost no
philosophers believe this anymore. Today, some still argue that suffering and
evil at least make it unlikely that God exists, **but there are good reasons to
keep believing in God despite all the evil and suffering."***

There's a lot we could say in response to the "slim chance" claim, but let's focus on two main responses.

First response: We usually can't know why God allows the suffering and evil that he does because our view of things is too limited. We only see part of the picture, but God sees all the details. This means we just can't know whether there's too much suffering or evil, and we can't be sure that certain sufferings are pointless.

Imagine you're looking at a huge picture, a beautiful piece of art made of thousands of different threads. But instead of seeing the whole picture, you can only see one tiny thread, and you can't step back far enough to see how all the threads fit together to create the whole picture. That's kind of like us—we only see a small part of life, but God sees the entire picture. He understands how everything fits together, even when we can't.

So, it's really not possible for us to be sure that there's too much suffering and evil in the world. It may seem to us like the world would be way better off if there were much less suffering and evil. But what if God knows that fewer people would turn to him and find salvation if the world had less suffering? Sometimes it's only when we go through hard times that we seek God and turn from sin. It's far more important that we accept God's grace and live forever with him than it is for us to be comfortable in this life (Romans 8:18; 2 Corinthians 4:17). So maybe God has a good reason to allow this much suffering.

And it's also impossible for us to know when suffering is pointless. A certain suffering may seem pointless to us, but what if God knows that it will lead to a chain of events that results in thousands of people coming to know Jesus and being saved years from now? There was no way that we could see how this one tragic event would eventually lead to so many people gaining eternal life. So, what seems pointless may not be pointless after all—it may lead to a great deal of good that we never could have predicted.

Second response: When we consider all of the evidence for God, we have good reason to believe in him. It's true that evil and suffering can lead us to doubt whether God exists. But what about all the good evidence *for* God?

Earlier in this book, we looked at a lot of good evidence for God and for Christianity. We have great evidence for the creation of the universe, the amazing design we see in the universe and living things, a powerful moral argument for God, and the strong case for the resurrection of Jesus. Each of these points provides strong support for the belief that God exists, even when evil and suffering challenge our faith.

Q. Read Romans 8:18 and 2 Corinthians 4:17. What do these verses tell us about what God cares about the most—our happiness forever or our comfort right now? How does the illustration of seeing just a tiny part (like a little thread) instead of the whole picture help us understand this?

3 Can you fill in the blanks from memory?

Can we believe in a powerful and loving God when the world has so much suffering and evil?

"Suffering and e___ (*evil*) make it hard for some to believe in G___ (*God*). It was once commonly claimed that suffering and evil d___ (*disprove*) God, but almost n___ (*no*) philosophers believe this anymore. Today, some still argue that suffering and evil at least make it u___ (*unlikely*) that God exists, but there are good r___ (*reasons*) to keep believing in God despite all the evil and suffering."

4 Continuing the Conversation . . .

Knowing: Using what you learned from this conversation, explain the difference between the "no way" claim and the "slim chance" claim. Can you give a response to each of these? It would be helpful to do a role play with someone who takes the view that suffering and evil make it hard to believe in God.

Doing: Watch one of the videos in the "Additional Resources" section below. Write down 1–3 things that you learned and discuss them with a parent or friend.

Sharing: Share what you learned in this conversation with a friend who struggles to believe in God because of suffering and evil. Another option is leading a small group discussion with friends or family members where you share what you've learned. Or you could share an insight or personal story about trusting God through suffering and evil with a friend or on social media.

5 Additional Resources

Scriptures & Print Resources:

- Scriptures: Psalm 34:18; Isaiah 55:8–9; John 9:1–3; John 16:32–33; Romans 8:18—25; Romans 11:33–34; 2 Corinthians 4:6–18; James 1:2–4, 12–15; Revelation 21:1–4
- Book: William Lane Craig, *On Guard: Defending Your Faith with Reason and Precision.* Colorado Springs: David C. Cook, 2010. See chapter 7 for a discussion of why God allows suffering and evil.

Online Resources:

Note: To link to these resources, click the QR code below or go to www.Renew.org/GC

- The Connection Pointe Worldview Website has a series on why God allows suffering and evil.
- Video: Zach Breitenbach gives a sermon at Connection Pointe Christian Church on how God fits with suffering and evil.
- Video: A ReasonableFaith.org animated video discusses the "no way" claim (also known as the logical problem of evil).
- Video: A ReasonableFaith.org animated video discusses the "slim chance" claim (also known as the evidential problem of evil).

- Article: Daniel McCoy, "Why Does God Allow Suffering?" This article explores the sources of suffering and asks what good reasons God might have for allowing suffering.

PRIVACY.FLOWCODE.COM

How do I deal with the anger and distrust I feel because of suffering and unanswered prayer?

1 **How would *you* answer the question, "How do I deal with the anger and distrust I feel because of suffering and unanswered prayer?"**

Here's the answer we'll explore:

> "Even if you believe God exists despite all the suffering in the world, suffering in your own life can make it hard to follow God—it can lead to anger at God or not trusting him. But Jesus suffered for you, and this can help you trust in God's love even when things don't make sense. Unanswered prayer can also make it feel like God is absent or doesn't care. But silence is not absence, and we have good reason to trust God's answers to prayer."

2 Now, let's walk through this answer . . .

Part 1: "Even if you believe God exists despite all the suffering in the <u>world</u>, suffering in your <u>own</u> life can make it hard to follow God . . ."

Brian and Amanda Bayers had tried to have a child for three and a half years. So when their son Jackson was born in 2013, they were overjoyed. But their joy turned to heartbreak on the morning of February 13, 2015. When Jackson was 18 months old, he tragically died after his dad accidentally backed over him with their truck.

This is just about the worst thing I can imagine—losing a child, especially when your own actions played a part in it. Both Brian and Amanda were devastated. When Amanda was interviewed by the local news, she said that right after losing her son, she just kept asking, "Why?"

It's in moments like these that trusting God can become incredibly hard. We all know that bad things happen in the world, and we may even have good reasons to believe God exists despite the suffering and evil around us. But when tragedy hits *your own life,* it can be hard to keep following God. There are many emotional challenges that make it difficult to hold on to faith when you're in the middle of intense pain and confusion.

Q. Have you (or maybe someone close to you) ever experienced suffering or loss that shook your faith in God? What were your feelings at that time?

*Part 2: "Even if you believe God exists despite all the suffering in the <u>world</u>,
suffering in your <u>own</u> life can make it hard to follow God—**it can lead to
<u>anger</u> at God or not trusting him** . . ."*

Even though there are good *general* answers to why God would allow suffering and evil
(see the previous conversation in this book), we almost never know the *specific* reason
that God allows a *certain* suffering to enter our lives. For example, *why did my aunt die
of cancer at a relatively young age?* I will never know God's exact reasons in this life. Why
didn't God keep little Jackson from dying? I don't know.

The pain we feel from these kinds of events, along with not knowing the specific reason
why God allowed them, can cause many different struggles in our relationship with him.
First, it can lead to anger at God—blaming him for allowing this to happen. Second, we
might start to doubt that God is good. We might think, "There may be a powerful Being
running the universe, but he isn't a good one." Third, it can lead to a loss of trust in God,
making us think, "If God let this happen, I can never trust him again." Fourth, you could
begin to believe that God doesn't love you. "Maybe he loves others," you might think, "but
he obviously doesn't care for me." Finally, it can cause you to avoid God—just wanting
nothing to do with him at all.

Q. Read Psalm 44. What does it teach you about the importance of expressing our
frustrations and pain to God? Do you think it is best to be honest with God about how
you feel in times like these, or should you keep it to yourself? Why?

Part 3: "Even if you believe God exists despite all the suffering in the _world_, suffering in your _own_ life can make it hard to follow God—it can lead to _anger_ at God or not trusting him. **But Jesus _suffered_ for you, and this can help you trust in God's love even when things don't make _sense_ . . ."**

Even though you won't always know the specific reasons why God allows certain sufferings in your life, there is a powerful reason to hold onto your love for God and your trust in him: Jesus proved God's love for you on the cross.

Jesus, who is God in human form, proved to us that we have a God who understands suffering. He didn't stop his own suffering. He didn't stay in the comfort of heaven and watch us struggle from a distance. Instead, God came into our world and experienced more pain than we will ever know. Even more than that, he did it for you and me. He was crucified for our sins and rebellion (Isaiah 53:5). Even though he never did anything wrong, it was God's plan for him to suffer for our guilt (Isaiah 53:9-10). He took the penalty for our sins—the curse—upon himself (Galatians 3:13). God has shown his love for us through what he has done: "God demonstrates his own love for us in this: While we were still sinners, Christ died for us" (Romans 5:8).

So, when we choose to keep trusting and loving God even when we don't understand some of the painful things in our lives, this is not blind faith. We have confidence in who God is—that he loves us and wants the best for us—because of what he has already done for us and what he has promised. It's like how a young child may not understand why her mom is letting her get a painful shot, but she trusts her mom because she has seen the evidence of her mom's love and care.

Also, remember that God has promised to take away all our pain, crying, and even death itself (Revelation 21:1–5). Jesus' resurrection is the proof that suffering and evil won't have the last word. There will be mysteries in this life, and things will hurt. But Jesus hurt, too. He shared in our suffering. He hurt for you and he loves you. And his death and resurrection are not just proof of God's love—they also prove that death has been defeated (1 Corinthians 15:54–57), and we can count on God's promise to end all our suffering. For those who trust Christ, death is just a transition to an infinitely better life. So hang in there a little longer. When Jesus returns, he will perfect our broken world and make everything perfect.

Q. What does Romans 5:8 mean to you when you are struggling with suffering? How can remembering Jesus' sacrifice on the cross help you trust God and love Him, even when you are hurting and don't have all the answers?

*Part 4: "Even if you believe God exists despite all the suffering in the world, suffering in your own life can make it hard to follow God—it can lead to anger at God or not trusting him. But Jesus suffered for you, and this can help you trust in God's love even when things don't make sense. **Unanswered prayer can also make it feel like God is absent or doesn't care . . ."***

But what about the times when I've prayed to God for certain things—even big things—and God didn't answer the way I asked? In fact, sometimes it felt like God was silent while I was going through something difficult.

Maybe there have been times when you poured out your heart to God, asking for help, guidance, or comfort, only to feel like your prayers weren't answered. The silence can feel deafening. In those moments, it's easy to wonder if God is really listening and if he cares about what you're going through. You might start to feel like he is distant, almost absent, leaving you to face your struggles on your own.

Q. Have you ever struggled with feeling like God is distant? Have you prayed for something important to you, but God didn't answer right away, or didn't answer in the way you had hoped? Explain.

Part 5: "Even if you believe God exists despite all the suffering in the <u>world</u>, suffering in your <u>own</u> life can make it hard to follow God—it can lead to <u>anger</u> at God or not trusting him. But Jesus <u>suffered</u> for you, and this can help you trust in God's love even when things don't make <u>sense</u>. Unanswered prayer can also make it feel like God is <u>absent</u> or doesn't care. **But <u>silence</u> is not absence, and we have good reason to <u>trust</u> God's answers to prayer."**

It's important to remember that silence doesn't mean absence. Just because God doesn't always answer immediately or in the way we expect, that doesn't mean he's not there or that he doesn't care.

If God is perfectly good and loving and is all-knowing, then we should expect that there will be times when his answer to our prayers isn't what we wanted. We are incredibly limited in what we understand. We can't see how one event will impact the world or what effect it will have on future generations. We also don't have all the information needed to make perfect decisions about what's best for us or others—or when things should happen. Plus, we're not perfectly good and loving. Our motives aren't always pure, even when we think they are.

Because of these limitations, we often will never fully understand why God didn't answer a prayer the way we wanted. But sometimes, later on, we may see why he answered the way he did. For example, Billy Graham had a dream of being a major league baseball player, but God had a much bigger plan for his life. Although falling short of his baseball dreams was disappointing to Graham at first, he later became one of the most powerful preachers of God's Word, leading millions of people to Jesus.

In my (Zach's) own life, I'm thankful that many of my prayers weren't answered as I had hoped. For years, I prayed for a spouse, but I didn't marry until I was 42. Although the waiting was difficult, I now see how much I grew during that time. And I wouldn't have met my incredible wife, Eva, or had our son, Paul, without that wait.

It's okay to be honest with God when he seems distant or when we don't understand his actions or his timing. But we should always trust that God's plans are better than ours. As Jesus said in his model prayer, we are to pray that God's will be done (Matthew 6:10). In Psalm 22, David begins with a cry of abandonment: "My God, my God, why have you forsaken me?" But by the end of the psalm, he says he still trusts in God's faithfulness. This is a great example for us. Remember that God's ways are higher than ours (Isaiah 55:8–9) and his timing is often different from ours (2 Peter 3:8–9). And even in the silence, God is always present with you (Psalm 139:7–10). His silence doesn't mean he's absent. Often, he's working in ways we don't fully understand, teaching us patience, improving our character, or preparing us for something better than we can imagine.

Q. Has there been a situation where you were disappointed with God's response to your prayer, only to see later how it worked out for your good? How can you grow in trusting God's plans even when you don't fully understand them?

3 Can you fill in the blanks from memory?

How do I deal with the anger and distrust I feel because of suffering and unanswered prayer?

"Even if you believe God exists despite all the s____ (*suffering*) in the world, suffering in your o____ (*own*) life can make it hard to follow God—it can lead to a____ (*anger*) at God or not trusting him. But Jesus s____ (*suffered*) for you, and this can help you trust in God's love even when things don't make s____ (*sense*). Unanswered prayer can also make it feel like God is a____ (*absent*) or doesn't care. But s____ (*silence*) is not absence, and we have good reason to t____ (*trust*) God's answers to prayer."

4 Continuing the Conversation . . .

Knowing: Read Psalm 13 and 22, two psalms of David. How does David feel at the beginning of these psalms? What is David's attitude at the end of these psalms? Think about your own life and experiences of suffering or unanswered prayer. How do they relate to the feelings David expresses in these psalms? What can you learn from David about expressing your feelings to God while still trusting him?

Doing: Write down a prayer of trust to God, following David's example in Psalm 13. Tell God your feelings about your struggles with suffering or unanswered prayers. If you want to trust in God's wisdom and timing, say that to God. End your prayer by asking God to guide you and help you follow his best plan for you.

Sharing: Share at least one key point that you took away from this conversation with a friend or family member. Encourage them to trust God in the midst of suffering or when prayers seem unanswered.

5 Additional Resources

Scriptures & Print Resources:

- Scriptures: Job 1:20–22; Psalm 13; Psalm 22; Psalm 34:18; Psalm 42:9–11; Psalm 44; Psalm 139:7–10; Isaiah 40:28–31; Isaiah 53; Isaiah 55:8–9; Romans 5:1–8; Romans 8:16–39; 1 Corinthians 15:54–57; 2 Corinthians 1:1–11; 2 Corinthians 12:7–9; Galatians 3:13; 2 Peter 3:8–9; Revelation 21:4
- Book: William Lane Craig, *On Guard: Defending Your Faith with Reason and Precision.* Colorado Springs: David C. Cook, 2010. See the part of chapter 7 that addresses the emotional problem of suffering and evil (pages 169-173).

Online Resources:

Note: To link to these resources, click the QR code below or go to www.Renew.org/GC

- The Connection Pointe Worldview Website discusses the emotional pain of evil.
- Video: Zach Breitenbach gives a sermon at Connection Pointe Christian Church that addresses the emotional problem of suffering and evil.
- William Lane Craig leads a Bible class on the emotional struggle with suffering.

- Article: Zach Breitenbach responds to a question about God's goodness on the "Room For Doubt" website from a parent who fears losing a child.
- Online Book: See chapter six ("When God Does Not Answer") of Gary Habermas's free online book *Dealing With Doubt*.

PRIVACY.FLOWCODE.COM

Is Jesus worth following even when it gets hard?

1 How would *you* answer the question, "Is Jesus worth following even when it gets hard?"

Here's the answer we'll explore:

> "Jesus is worthy of our allegiance to the end because he alone is worthy to defeat evil and restore creation. Even when life gets hard, Jesus' kingdom stays standing."

2 Now, let's walk through this answer.

Part 1: "Jesus is <u>worthy</u> . . ."

Who is worthy? That sounds like a Bible question—and it is–but it's also a question that millions of us ask every day. Every four years in November, millions of Americans cast their vote for who they think is worthy to be President. Basketball fans debate who is worthy to be the NBA's most valuable player each year. Award shows such as the Golden Globes and the Oscars announce which actor, actress, film, or film score is the most worthy to receive the award that year. And on reality competition shows, millions of viewers debate who is most worthy to be crowned the best chef, athlete, or survivalist.

In the book of Revelation, we get a glimpse into a powerful scene in heaven where an angel asks this same question, "Who is worthy?" There's a scroll that contains God's plan for defeating evil, and the big question on everybody's mind is: Who is worthy to open it? The author of Revelation, John, weeps because it seems like no one is worthy. But then one of the elders points out that there is one who is worthy:

> "Then one of the elders said to me, 'Do not weep! See, the Lion of the tribe of Judah, the Root of David, has triumphed. He is able to open the scroll and its seven seals.'" (Revelation 5:5)

These titles—the Lion of the tribe of Judah, the Root of David—are titles of Jesus. And even though people will continue to debate who is most worthy of this award or that high responsibility, the Bible clearly answers the most important question of all: Only Jesus is worthy to carry out God's plan, defeat evil, and fully deserve our trust.

Q. What is it about Jesus that makes him the one worthy to defeat evil?

Part 2: "Jesus is worthy of our allegiance to the end . . ."

Do you know how much people pay for weddings these days? Depending on the location, it might be anywhere from $20,000 to $50,000—just for this one-day event. Unless you're ridiculously wealthy, that's a ton of money. And yet we've probably all heard of people who had impressive weddings—but then their marriage sadly crumbled not long after. The truth is, the most important thing was never the *event;* it's the actual relationship. But people can sadly focus way more on planning the perfect wedding and barely prepare at all for the marriage itself.

In the same way, salvation isn't just a one-time event; it's a lifelong relationship. A lot of people put all the emphasis on the event of "getting saved," but not much emphasis on what salvation is all about: their lifelong relationship with God. We need to be reminded that faith is for the long haul.

Starting strong isn't the main thing that matters. Staying close to God is. And Psalm 86 helps us understand what a *lifelong* relationship with God looks like.

First, check out Psalm 86:2–4. It describes someone who's committed to staying faithful to God:

> "Guard my life, for I am faithful to you; save your servant who trusts in you. You are my God; have mercy on me, Lord, for I call to you all day long. Bring joy to your servant, Lord, for I put my trust in you." (Psalm 86:2–4)

That's the kind of heart we want to have: someone who's committed to trusting God. But how exactly do we stay faithful to God when we struggle to be consistent? Psalm 86 answers that too. It's because of *God's* faithfulness to us. The psalmist continues by praying,

> "Teach me your way, Lord, that I may rely on your faithfulness; give me an undivided heart, that I may fear your name....But you, Lord, are a compassionate and gracious God, slow to anger, abounding in love and faithfulness." (Psalm 86:11, 15)

Jesus is worthy of our allegiance all the way to the end. And even when we mess up or stumble, we can stay faithful to him because he always remains faithful to us.

Q. Who is someone you know who remained faithful to Jesus all the way to death? Is there anything you can learn from their life?

*Part 3: "Jesus is <u>worthy</u> of our <u>allegiance</u> to the <u>end</u> **because he alone is worthy to defeat <u>evil</u> and restore <u>creation</u>**. . . ."*

So, why is Jesus worthy of our full allegiance—our lifelong commitment? That's a big ask, right? If someone is going to ask for your total commitment, there better be a good reason. So let's go back to that moment in Revelation, where someone in heaven asks, "Who is worthy to break the seals and open the scroll?" (Revelation 5:2b). The scroll holds God's plan to defeat evil. And the only one found worthy to open it is called the "Lion of the Tribe of Judah, the Root of David."

So, John turns to look, probably expecting to see a powerful, majestic lion. Instead, he sees something very surprising. John writes, "Then I saw a Lamb, looking as if it had been slain, standing at the center of the throne" (Revelation 5:6a).

Well, that's a real plot twist. How did something as humble as a lamb—a sacrificed lamb, no less—triumph? How did a *lamb* win the throne? What made a sacrificed lamb worthy to break the seals and open the scroll?

In heaven, everyone watches as the Lamb reaches out and takes hold of the scroll. As he takes it, everyone falls on their faces before the Lamb, and they sing a song that goes like this:

> "You are worthy to take the scroll and to open its seals, because you were slain, and with your blood you purchased for God persons from every tribe and language and people and nation. You have made them to be a kingdom and priests to serve our God, and they will reign on the earth." (Revelation 5:9–10)

More and more voices join the song, until millions upon millions of angels are singing,

"Worthy is the Lamb, who was slain, to receive power and wealth and wisdom and strength and honor and glory and praise!" (Revelation 5:12)

So why is Jesus worthy of our total allegiance–our full commitment until the end? As these songs tell us, he is worthy because he was slain, and with his blood he purchased us back for God. The Bible word for buying something back is "redeem." Jesus redeemed us from our slavery to sin and death, so that we can be part of his kingdom. We get to be his sons and daughters, reigning with him forever. Jesus Christ became like us so that we can become like him.

What's the only response that makes sense? To join the song in heaven and say with everything we've got: "Jesus is worthy! He's worthy of our full allegiance for all our days."

Q. An Old English word we don't use anymore is "worth-ship." It meant "worthiness" or "honor" or "dignity." Eventually the English language changed and "worth-ship" was shortened to the word "worship." When we *worship* God, we're telling him that he has ultimate worth; we're also living like he's worthy. Why is worshiping God so important for our maturity as disciples of Jesus?

*Part 4: "Jesus is <u>worthy</u> of our <u>allegiance</u> to the <u>end</u> because he alone is <u>worthy</u> to defeat <u>evil</u> and restore <u>creation</u>. **Even when life gets <u>hard</u>**...*"

We might want to pause and think about all that Jesus went through—the betrayal, floggings, crucifixion, loneliness, mockery, and death—in order to buy us back from our slavery to sin and death. Apparently, Jesus saw us as worth saving even when it got hard for him. In turn, as his disciples, we see him as worth following even when it gets hard for us.

The early Christians understood this. Because of their faith, we read about some of them being exiled (Revelation 1:9), flogged (Acts 5:40), stoned (2 Corinthians 11:25), beheaded

(Acts 12:2), and even crucified (John 21:18–19). And around the world today, many Christians still face these sorts of sufferings.

Meanwhile, in the Western world, where both of us are writing from, Christians often get really scared over much milder sufferings, such as being looked down on or perhaps made fun of for our faith. That might seem somewhat understandable; after all, no one likes being insulted or excluded. And yet, how does Jesus say we should feel when we are mistreated because of our faith? He says:

> "You are blessed when they insult and persecute you and falsely say every kind of evil against you because of me. Be glad and rejoice, because your reward is great in heaven. For that is how they persecuted the prophets who were before you." (Matthew 5:11–12).

Come again? Yeah, Jesus actually said we should feel blessed when people treat us badly for following him. And, clearly, Jesus' disciples fully bought into this idea; many of them suffered greatly for their faith. His disciple Peter wrote, "But even if you should suffer for righteousness, you are blessed" (1 Peter 3:14a).

There is something powerful and honorable about going through hardship for a good cause. And when we say that Jesus is worthy, we are also saying that he is worthy of our trust and loyalty—even when it gets hard.

Q. Have you experienced difficulties following Jesus? Have those difficulties made you more determined or less determined to follow him?

*Part 5: "Jesus is <u>worthy</u> of our <u>allegiance</u> to the <u>end</u> because he alone is <u>worthy</u> to defeat <u>evil</u> and restore <u>creation</u>. Even when life gets <u>hard</u>, **<u>Jesus' kingdom stays standing.</u>**"*

All it takes is a phone call from a relative about an accident. Or some chilling words you didn't expect to hear in a routine checkup. All it takes is four words: "This marriage is over." Or another four words: "The tumor is malignant." Or another four words: "I got laid off."

Sometimes your world is going to shake.

You'll get reminders throughout your life—little rumblings that get louder and louder—that, in the end, everything gets shaken. Christians have always believed that there will be an end to history—that it's moving toward a final moment. We talk about the return of Jesus. We talk about Judgment Day. And when that day comes, what will still be left standing? The stuff we've built? All the money we've made? All the health we've enjoyed? All the insurance we've bought? In the end, none of that is left standing. Everything gets shaken. At that final earthquake, everything comes tumbling down.

But not everything falls. Read the scripture below to find out the one thing that remains. When political leaders fail to deliver on their promises, when sin fails to satisfy us, when our projects fail, or when our health falls apart—it's painful, but it can also be powerful. How? Because all these disappointments become invitations to trust God. Hebrews 12:28–29 says, "Therefore, since we are receiving a kingdom that cannot be shaken, let us be thankful, and so worship God acceptably with reverence and awe, for our 'God is a consuming fire.'"

Even when life feels like it's crumbling apart, Jesus' kingdom stays standing.

Q. Read Hebrews 12:28–29 again. When everything in your life feels shaken (your plans, your security, your health, etc.), what are you standing on that can't be shaken? Are you building your life on something that will last when everything else falls?

3 Can you fill in the blanks from memory?

Is Jesus worth following even when it gets hard?

"Jesus is w____ (*worthy*) of our a____ (*allegiance*) to the e____ (*end*) because he alone is w____ (*worthy*) to defeat e____ (*evil*) and restore c____ (*creation*). Even when life gets h____ (*hard*), Jesus' k____ (*kingdom*) stays s____ (*standing*)."

4 Continuing the Conversation . . .

Knowing: Think about your favorite hero from a movie, book, or real life. What kind of battles do they fight and win? Now compare that to the battles Jesus fights for us: battles to defeat sin, Satan, and death. Why is Jesus the only hero who can truly win the fight that matters most?

Doing: Sometimes we think of "worship" as primarily something we do at church, usually by singing songs. And yes, singing worship songs to God is a very good and biblical thing. But worship is a lot more than just singing. And it's certainly more than the inspirational feeling many of us get when we sing beautiful music. Next time you're singing worship songs at church, don't just focus on the music (if that's what you find yourself focusing on). *Use that moment to offer your whole life to God.* Remember Romans 12:1, where Paul says true worship is being a living sacrifice. As you sing, tell God with your heart and actions that he's worthy of more than just your voice; he's worthy of how you live every day.

Sharing: If you know somebody who is discouraged by the way the world shakes around them, ask to pray for them. And encourage them with the truth that, whatever shakes in our world, Jesus' kingdom stands strong.

5 Additional Resources

Scriptures & Print Resources:

- Scriptures: Revelation 5; Psalm 86; Matthew 5:11–12; 1 Peter 3:14–16; Hebrews 12:28–29
- Book: Kelvin Teamer, *Kingdom Life: Experiencing God's Reign Through Love and Holiness,* Renew.org, 2021. This short book explains what God's kingdom really means and shows how you can live as part of it in today's world.
- Book: Tony Twist and Mihai Malancea, *Grand Metanarrative: God's Story as an Invitation to Theology,* Renew.org, 2021. This short book summarizes the grand story of the Bible. We can follow Jesus faithfully in light of the story's end and the renewal Jesus is bringing.

Online Resources:

Note: To link to these resources, click the QR code below or go to www.Renew.org/GC

- Article: G. W. Steel, "What Was Jesus' Teaching? Rediscovering Jesus' Primary Message." This article reminds us of the core teaching of Jesus' earthly ministry, as he invited us to repent and place faith in the good news of his kingdom.

PRIVACY.FLOWCODE.COM

Notes

[1] C. S. Lewis, *The Problem of Pain* (San Francisco: Harper San Francisco, 2001), 18.

[2] Galileo Galilei, *The Assayer,* 1623, in *Discoveries and Opinions of Galileo,* edited and translated by Stillman Drake, 237–38 (New York: Anchor Books, 1957), 183–184.

[3] Fred Hoyle, "The Universe: Past and Present Reflections," *Engineering and Science* 45 (November, 1981), 8–12. The quote is on page 12.

[4] Antony Flew, *There Is a God: How the World's Most Notorious Atheist Changed His Mind,* with Roy Abraham Varghese (New York: HarperOne, 2007), 88.

[5] Bill Gates, *The Road Ahead,* Rev. ed. (New York: Penguin Books, 1996), 228.

[6] Richard Dawkins, *The God Delusion* (London: Bantam Publishers, 2006), 125.

[7] Richard Dawkins, *The Blind Watchmaker: Why the Evidence of Evolution Reveals a Universe Without Design* (New York: W. W. Norton & Company, 1996), 6.

[8] Dawkins, *The God Delusion,* 132.

[9] Some might argue that the fine-tuning could be explained by the multiverse theory, where multiple universes exist with different conditions. We didn't address this theory here, as it lacks empirical support and does not eliminate the need for a fine-tuner. For a good summary on why this is the case, see Willian Lane Craig, "Has the Multiverse Replaced God?" *Reasonable Faith,* https://www.reasonablefaith.org/writings/popular-writings/existence-nature-ofgod/has-the-multiverse-replaced-god.

[10] Bart D. Ehrman, *Did Jesus Exist?: The Historical Argument for Jesus of Nazareth* (New York: HarperOne, 2012), 12.

[11] Ehrman, Did Jesus Exist?, 156–164, 290–291.

[12] See *Josephus's Antiquities of the Jews* Book 4, Chapter 8.

[13] It's clear that Paul is quoting another source because he starts off in verse 3 by saying he's passing on what he also received. And the style of this passage is rhythmic and easy-to-memorize, which is typical of creeds. Also, note that the book of 1 Corinthians is one of the letters of Paul that virtually no scholar disputes was actually written by Paul.

[14] Paul received this information no later than his trip to Jerusalem, just three years after his conversion (Galatians 1:18-19), and his conversion was about two years after Jesus died.

[15] "The Twelve" was a title used to refer to Jesus' disciples even though Judas, one of the twelve disciples, had died.

[16] Bart D. Ehrman, *Jesus, Interrupted: Revealing the Hidden Contradictions in the Bible (And Why We Don't Know About Them)* (New York: HarperOne, 2009), 177. When Ehrman says Paul was writing about 25 years later, this refers to the book of 1 Corinthians. But even though 1 Corinthians was written about 25 years after Jesus died, Ehrman admits Paul met these witnesses very early (within a few years after Jesus died) and there is good reason to believe they really claimed to see appearances of Jesus.

[17] Winfried Corduan, *Neighboring Faiths: A Christian Introduction to World Religions,* third edition (Downers Grove, InterVarsity Press, 2024), 16.

[18] Aleksandr Solzhenitsyn, "Acceptance Address by Mr. Aleksandr Solzhenitsyn," *Templeton Prize,* May 10, 1983, https://www.templetonprize.org/laureate-sub/solzhenitsyn-acceptance-speech/.

[19] I am indebted for this illustration to Ozark Christian College professor of New Testament Kenny Boles.

[20] The technical name for this argument that we are calling the "no way" claim is the "logical problem of evil." It's called this because the argument is that God and suffering/evil are logically incompatible.

[21] Plantinga's argument is called the Free Will Defense, and he made his case in the following book: *God, Freedom, and Evil* (Grand Rapids, MI: Eerdmans, 1974).

[22] The technical name for this argument that we are calling the "slim chance" claim is the "evidential problem of evil." It's called this because it focuses on the evidence of suffering and evil in the world and argues that the existence of such evil makes it unlikely (but not necessarily impossible) that an all-powerful, all-good God exists.

About the Authors

Daniel McCoy is happily married to Susanna, and they have 3 daughters and 2 sons. He is the editorial director for Renew.org as well as a professor-at-large of philosophy for Ozark Christian College. He has a bachelor's in theology (Ozark Christian College), master of arts in apologetics (Veritas International University), and PhD in theology (North-West University, South Africa). Among his books are the *Popular Handbook of World Religions* (general editor), *Real Life Theology Handbook* (with Andrew Jit), and *The Atheist's Fatal Flaw* (co-authored with Norman Geisler).

Zach Breitenbach is Director of Content & Curriculum in the Worldview Ministry at Connection Pointe Christian Church in central Indiana, equipping youth and adults to engage with biblical truth thoughtfully and faithfully. He holds a Ph.D. in Theology and Christian Apologetics from Liberty University and has taught theology, philosophy, and apologetics at the high school, undergraduate, and seminary levels. Dr. Breitenbach writes Connection Pointe's Worldview teaching resources (https://worldview.cp.church/series), has published numerous articles, and authored the book *Slipping Through the Cracks*. His passion is helping people—especially youth—understand, defend, and live out their faith with confidence in everyday life.

www.ingramcontent.com/pod-product-compliance
Lightning Source LLC
Chambersburg PA
CBHW081131090426
42737CB00018B/3291